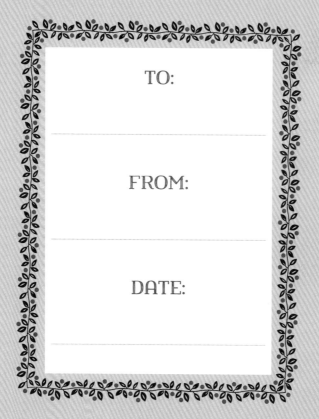

TO:

FROM:

DATE:

PRAISE FOR
*YOU CAN STAY HOME
WITH YOUR KIDS!*

"I can still remember the day I took a big leap of faith and quit my full-time job to stay home with my first child. It was the best decision I ever made, but it sure wasn't easy. Packed with invaluable tips and tricks to make this dream a reality, *You Can Stay Home with Your Kids!* would have saved me so much time *and* money! I wish I had this book fifteen years ago, but I found many things I could implement even now. It is pure gold!"

Ruth Schwenk, founder of TheBetterMom.com and
author of *Pressing Pause* and *The Better Mom*

"Erin's huge, compassionate heart for moms comes through loud and clear on each page of this hopeful, life-giving book. For anyone wishing to stay home who is just not sure it's a realistic dream, Erin's practical tips and experience makes the impossible feel within reach!"

Jamie C. Martin, author of *Give Your Child the World*
and cofounder of SimpleHomeschool.net

"As a mom who stayed home with her kids, I can testify that Erin Odom packs into her book wisdom and practical ideas that work. Her suggestions for curtailing spending, uncovering ways to save, and creatively looking for opportunities to earn a side hustle offer hope and direction for moms in all seasons and stages of motherhood."

Elisa Pulliam, author of *Meet the New You*, life coach and mentor, and founder of MoretoBe.com

"I loved *More Than Just Making It* for the glimpse into Erin's life and heart. In *You Can Stay Home With Your Kids!* the focus turns practical—my favorite! I have absolutely no doubt that if you buy this book and implement just a few ideas, you will earn your money back . . . and so much more!"

Jessica Smartt, creator of smarttereachday.com and upcoming author with Thomas Nelson

"If staying home with your kids sounds like a luxury you can't afford, Erin's practical action steps will pave a way through many of the obstacles standing in your way. It takes creativity, intentionality, and determination, but by putting into practice many of the insightful tips and tricks that Erin shares, I was able to stay home with our five children, and you can do it too. If you've ever pondered ways to slash your budget to allow more freedom and flexibility, start here. *You Can Stay Home with Your Kids!* is a treasure trove of wisdom you don't want to miss."

Jen Schmidt, family manager behind *Balancing Beauty and Bedlam*, author of *Just Open the Door*, and host of The Becoming Conference

"I thought I'd pulled out all the stops to stay home with my kids, but I haven't done even half the ways Erin shares here! If you would love to stay home with your kid, this book is an investment in that dream."

Rachel Norman, mom of five and founder of the
popular blog *A Mother Far from Home*

"Erin Odom doesn't just tell us why staying home with our kids is important (we've read that book before), but she suggests ways to actually *do* it! If you're ready to go from the principle of being a stay-at-home mom to the practical reality of making it work, this is the book for you!

Wendy Speake, author of *Triggers*, *Parenting Scripts*,
and *Life Creative*

"*You Can Stay Home with Your Kids!* is an empowering read! As one who has made major life changes (and sacrifices) in order to stay home with my children, I affirm and resonate with the wisdom and inspiration offered in this book. If being at home is a desire of your heart, a little frugality and creativity just might be the keys that unlock that door. If there is a way to pull this off, Erin will help you find it!"

Katie Bennett, creator of the *Embracing a Simpler Life*
blog and podcast and author of *Heavenly Minded Mom*

YOU CAN STAY HOME WITH YOUR KIDS!

YOU CAN STAY HOME WITH YOUR KIDS!

100 TIPS, TRICKS, AND WAYS
TO MAKE IT WORK ON A BUDGET

ERIN ODOM

OF *THE HUMBLED HOMEMAKER* BLOG

ZONDERVAN®

ZONDERVAN

You Can Stay Home with Your Kids!
Copyright © 2018 by Erin Odom

Requests for information should be addressed to:
Zondervan, 3900 Sparks Dr. SE, Grand Rapids, Michigan 49546

ISBN 978-0-3100-8356-6

Published in association with William K. Jensen Literary Agency, 119 Bampton Court, Eugene, Oregon 97404.

Art direction: Adam Hill
Interior design: Denise Froehlich

Printed in China

18 19 20 21 22 /TIMS/ 10 9 8 7 6 5 4 3 2

*To Mom, for staying at home
with my siblings and me*

———————————

*And to Daddy, for supporting
Mama and making it possible for
her to stay at home with her kids*

The year was 2008, and I desperately wanted to quit my job to stay home with our newborn daughter. My own mother made a career out of motherhood, and although she worked part-time until I was close to two years old, I don't remember a time when she wasn't a stay-at-home mom. I aspired for my children to know the same. But the 2008 economic crisis coincided with the birth of our first child. Because my husband, Will, was in school and working part-time at our church and our house had sunk underwater and was not selling, we were relying heavily on my income and the health insurance from my job. I had no other choice but to return to full-time work outside of the home when our daughter was just six weeks old.

I'll never forget leaving my newborn sitting in her swing the first morning I went back to work. Sound asleep after falling into a nursing coma, she was blissfully unaware that this would be the first time we would be separated since God began weaving her together in my womb. My trusted friend Lexie came over to babysit, so I knew my sweet girl was in good hands. Still, saying good-bye to my baby tore at my heart.

I worked full-time outside of the home until my daughter was six months old, and from then until she was nine months old, I attended missionary training classes while she stayed in a daycare-like setting. I know my time as a full-time, work-outside-the-home mom was a blip on the radar compared to so many mothers who desire to stay home with their children, but it still wasn't easy. I could have wallowed in self-pity for "missing out" on most of my daughter's first year of life, but I don't look back with regret; instead, I think about all God taught me—and how He provided for our family.

MORE THAN JUST MAKING IT

When our daughter was thirteen months old, we moved across the continent—from the Vancouver area of British Columbia, Canada, to the town in North Carolina where I grew up. Our family was struggling through some difficult circumstances, and we wanted to be close to my parents. My husband accepted a low-paying job as a high school Spanish teacher, and we decided to try making our pennies stretch enough for me to be a stay-at-home mom. At the time, we didn't even own a vehicle, but we were determined to make it work.

> My time as a full-time, work-outside-the-home mom was a blip on the radar compared to so many mothers who desire to stay home with their children, but it still wasn't easy.

My mother is a coupon queen, so I started clipping coupons myself. I learned to cook from scratch. We cut cable. We stopped eating out. And I made it my mission to spend as little money as possible. Still, we never seemed to make ends meet.

After taking a financial planning class and having our teacher pore over our bank statements and evaluate our spending habits, we learned that we simply didn't make enough money to live. Either I needed to go back to work full time, Will needed to secure a higher-paying job, or we needed to find some way for me to generate an income from home.

> I learned to cook from scratch. We cut cable. We stopped eating out. And I made it my mission to spend as little money as possible. Still, we never seemed to make ends meet.

By that time, our firstborn was more than three years old. We also had another daughter, who was then a toddler, and I was expecting our third. My determination to be a stay-at-home mom only intensified with each new child we added to our family. In my first book, *More Than Just Making It: Hope for the Heart of the Financially Frustrated*, I chronicle this often grueling time in our journey. Though an extremely difficult season, it was one in which we experienced God's provision like never before.

In *More Than Just Making It*, I explained what Will and I discovered during our season of financial frustration: those who struggle with money often have one of two problems—an income problem or a spending problem. Those with an income problem simply don't earn enough money to live. Those with a spending problem don't know how to steward their money wisely. The good news is, my friend, there is hope for both.

HOPE FOR STAYING HOME

In this book I hope to arm you with tips on how to both curb spending *and* create more income so that you can achieve your dream of staying home with your kids. Perhaps you are already a stay-at-home mom who lives with the daily tension of a bank account that never balances. Your family is up to your necks in debt, and cutting coupons just isn't cutting it. You need more money-saving tips—in bite-size chunks—to learn how to cut costs. You also want to discover some ways you can start bringing in a little extra money without leaving home. Friend, this book is for you.

> Those who struggle with money often have one of two problems—an income problem or a spending problem.

Or maybe you're still working outside of the home, and you feel God calling you to leave the workforce and become the stay-at-home mom you dream of being. You dread going to work each day, and you're tired of simply wishing you could be home with your kids— you want to make that a reality. Friend, this book is for you as well.

You may think there is no way you can afford to stay home with your kids, but often the adage is true: when there is a will, there *is* a way.

I won't pretend the following method will work for everyone, but for those who want to stay home with their kids, I recommend this three-step process:

Pay off all debts. Yes, I know some moms manage to stay home with their kids even though their families are tens of thousands of dollars in debt. But I promise you that you'll feel so much freedom when the noose of unpaid loans, credit cards, medical bills, and more is loosened, and you are able to pour one hundred percent of your income into your family's current and future needs (and maybe even a few wants). While this isn't a book about becoming debt-free, I encourage you to use the money-saving tips found in these pages and put those savings toward paying off all debts until they are gone. Once they are, you will be able to use that saved money toward other goals—like staying home with your kids!

Curb spending. Those of us who grew up in the 1980s and 1990s often look at the American dream as synonymous with "keeping up with the Joneses." Instead of operating out of our own convictions to achieve personal goals and individual callings, we've depleted our savings accounts, dug ourselves into debt, and burdened our emotional and mental capacities with stress that comes with our American cultural leaning toward excess. But you don't have to do that anymore! You can realize the freedom of living within your means and practicing contentment.

Create more income. I'm not here to preach that every single mother should stay home with her children or that those who work outside of the home are somehow doing their families a disservice. To the contrary, I encourage grace toward *all* mothers—no matter if they are working, staying at home, or practicing some kind of hybrid to help care for the needs of their families. But if you are either a stay-at-home mom who can barely afford it or if you're a working mom who knows your family can't survive without your income, my hope is that arming you with some ways to create more income *from home* will help make your dream of staying home with your kids a reality—or at least help alleviate some of the stress of living solely on your husband's income.

> I encourage grace toward *all* mothers—no matter if they are working, staying at home, or practicing some kind of hybrid to help care for the needs of their families.

HOW THIS BOOK WORKS

I've divided this book into eight sections: Curb Spending, Eat Well on a Budget, DIY Household Products, Entertain Your Family Without Spending a Fortune, Shop Secondhand and Sales, Provide for Health-Care Needs, Hunt Houses and Vehicles, and Create More Income. In each of these sections, you'll find tips for ways to stretch your money further than you ever imagined. Each tip ends with an action step that you can begin applying to your life.

My hope is that the extra money you're able to save and create will help you stay home with your kids. You might learn that you actually spend less money when you are home with your kids when you factor in the costs of childcare expenses, work clothes, gas, and lunches out—not to mention the time you save by not commuting to and from work. This time can also translate into money—as you will soon find out in the pages of this book.

Now, let's embark on this journey of learning how you can afford to be a stay-at-home mom. I'm praying for you and cheering you on all the way!

If you struggle with overspending, you are not alone. I have good news: you *can* learn to better steward your money! In this section we will explore ways you can curb spending in a variety of areas. If you want to make staying at home with your kids work, the goal is to live at or below your means. The truth is, you can usually live on a lot less money than you think, and living on less than you make will enable you to achieve greater dreams down the road because of the money you save in the process.

Will and I saved very little money during the first few years we were married. The ironic thing is that it was one of the richest seasons of our lives because we were both working full-time. Hindsight is twenty-twenty, but in retrospect, we should have been saving one hundred percent of my income. I cringe when I look back and think about how this would have enabled me to become a stay-at-home mom much sooner!

LIVE ON A BUDGET

While some people may see a budget as constraining, I find it liberating. In fact, I'm convinced there is no better way to gain financial freedom than by living within a budget. Budgeting can be the tool that removes the shackles from a spender's self-imposed prison of impulse purchases.

Budgeting has many benefits, but these are three of my favorites:

Budgeting helps you know how you're spending your money. Have you ever started the month with a full checking account but got to the end of the month and wondered, *Where did all the money go?* It's impossible to know if you're spending too much on food, clothing, or entertainment if you aren't keeping track of what you're spending and where you're spending it.

Budgeting helps you meet financial goals. Frivolous spending can take the place of fruitful savings—even when you don't realize it. It's difficult to meet long-term financial goals, like buying a house or a car, when you're living paycheck to paycheck. Having a proper budget in place will help you stop living month to month and achieve financial stability to plan for the future.

Budgeting helps bring freedom. Living within a budget frees you to do more of the things that matter most because you have total control of your money. A budget gives you the liberty to save for big financial goals, but it also allows you to spend the money you've allotted when a need (or even a want!) arises.

ACTION STEP: Research how to set up a basic budget. (I include a full chapter on budgeting in my book *More Than Just Making It*, but you can find many other budgeting resources available online.) The first step is to record your spending habits for one month. From there, you can better evaluate how much money you're spending—and which areas you can cut to save more.

TAKE A FINANCIAL PLANNING CLASS

Will and I took a financial planning class the first year we were married. I wish I could say we have been financially successful ever since, but the truth is that we walked through some extreme financial difficulties even after that class. If you don't see your situation improving after your first financial planning class, then take another!

I learned that gathering information without taking action gets you nowhere. Good ideas remain just that—ideas—until you take what you've learned and begin to apply them to your life.

Where can you take financial planning classes? Many churches and community groups offer these. Two curricula I recommend are Crown Financial Ministries (crown.org) and Dave Ramsey's Financial Peace University (daveramsey.com/fpu). That said, these classes may come with an investment—usually the cost of materials. If you cannot afford a financial planning class, seek out any available scholarships the hosting organization may offer. If those aren't available, check out financial planning books from your local library, or begin devouring one of many finance blogs or YouTube channels. My favorite finance blogs are moneysavingmom.com and seedtime.com. Dave Ramsey's website and podcast also offer a plethora of information for free. Any of these are worthwhile investments in both time and any financial resources you might have.

ACTION STEP: If you've never taken a financial planning class, make a plan to do so, stat! Search local church websites for upcoming classes. If you cannot afford a class, check out one of the blogs I mentioned or borrow books from the library.

MEET WITH A FINANCIAL PLANNER

More than anything else, meeting with a financial planner helped our family learn how to go from financial stress to financial success. We weren't able to turn our situation around—and feel fully confident in the decision for me to stay home with our kids—until we got to the root cause of our financial frustration. (In our case, it was a low income.)

Will and I found our financial planner at our church. He was the teacher of a financial planning class we had taken, and he volunteered his time to come to our home, pore over our finances, and help us make a plan.

Both Crown Financial Ministries and Financial Peace University offer a listing of local financial planning coaches online. Pastors or other church leaders also might offer financial planning help. Some financial planners are free, but others offer their services for a small fee. When you meet with a financial planner, be sure to share your goals—for you to stay home with your kids or to create more financial breathing room so that you can continue to do so.

ACTION STEP: If you attend church, send an e-mail to your pastor to ask about any recommendations for local financial planners. Or visit crown.org or daveramsey.com and search for financial planners in your area.

COMMUNICATE SPENDING WITH YOUR SPOUSE

Not only can overspending diminish your bank account, but it can also hurt your marriage—especially if your spouse doesn't know you're spending money. Will and I saw this early in our marriage; I was the saver, and he was the spender. We could have avoided many arguments if we had simply communicated about our spending.

We've found two ways to better communicate about money:

Budget or communication meetings. Will and I seek to meet to discuss our budget no less than once per month. We have other friends who have a weekly communication meeting. They have a regular babysitter who watches their four children while they go out to coffee and discuss their budget, family calendar, parenting challenges, and more. They have seen these regular times of intentional communication not only bolster their bank accounts but also strengthen their marriage.

A budgeting app. While many financial experts will laud the benefits of a cash-only budget, Will and I (and many others in our generation) opt for electronic bill paying, which is convenient but impossible to do with a cash-only budget. Because it can be easy to overspend when we don't have the cash on hand to remind us of what we have left in our bank account, we've chosen to use a budgeting app that acts like a real-time digital "envelope system." Will and I share the app so we can see what the other person spends. The system we use is called Mvelopes, but YNAB (You Need a Budget), EveryDollar, and Mint are three other highly regarded apps. Some apps are free, and some come with a small monthly fee.

The most important part? Both spouses must check the apps. They won't work if you don't use them!

ACTION STEP: Approach your spouse about scheduling regular budget or communication meetings. Select a date and put your first meeting on the calendar! Then, at your first meeting, research budgeting apps together and select one you want to try.

CURTAIL CREDIT CARD USE

I got my first credit card in college. It seemed like everyone else had one, so I got one too. I clearly remember swiping that card at Walmart for the first time. Even as I signed the receipt, I thought to myself, *What's the point?* I had enough money in my bank account, so I could have used my debit card. Why did I delay payment by using this other piece of plastic?

If you're trying to make it on one income in order to stay home with your kids, it can be tempting to use credit cards when money is tight. I encourage you to fight that temptation.

Credit cards are not evil in and of themselves. They can help build credit, and some people use them savvily to build up gas, airline, and even cash-back rewards. But for those who aren't disciplined enough to pay off the cards every month, using them can open the door to financial ruin.

Some people like to have at least one credit card on hand to use in case of an emergency. (My family doesn't regularly use credit cards, but we do have them for this reason. However, I don't recall ever using mine in the past decade—or even longer!) My suggestion is to keep your credit cards in a safe place in your home but *not in your wallet.* This will help curtail the temptation to use the credit cards for things you really can't afford to buy. Staying out of debt will give you the financial freedom to stay home with your kids.

ACTION STEP: Spend some time evaluating whether you need every credit card you have. Don't forget store credit cards. Be honest with yourself about which cards are more tempting to use. Then take a few hours to tally up your current credit card debt. Are you in over your head? Make a commitment to paying off the debt and curtailing future credit card use. Pay off the card with the smallest balance first. Releasing yourself from small debts will give you the confidence and courage to continue knocking down the credit card debt until it's all gone!

DISTINGUISH WANTS FROM NEEDS

One of the biggest financial faux pas Americans make is defining *wants* as *needs*. Our culture is spoiled with excess. We think we need a home that provides each child his or her own room. We think we need a new vehicle every few years. We think we need to outfit our wardrobes with the latest trends and stock our pantries with pricey snack foods. We think our children need to be involved in expensive extracurricular activities or they will never grow up to become well-rounded adults.

The truth is, we don't need any of these. Much of what we see as needs the rest of the world lives without. We can live without a lot if we exercise self-control.

You might enjoy cable television, the latest smartphone, and stainless steel appliances, but they aren't necessary for your survival. Food, water, shelter, basic clothing, and electricity are.

Start curbing spending by eliminating wants from your budget. This will help give you the financial breathing room you need to stay home with your kids. This is not to say that you should cut *all* wants from your budget, but even eliminating some line items can really add up.

ACTION STEP: Look over your bank statements from the past month. What are some areas of spending you've designated as *needs* that are really *wants*? Which of these are you willing to forgo to give your family more financial freedom? Record these, and set a date with your spouse to discuss cutting these wants from your budget.

WAIT BEFORE BUYING

The true test of knowing whether you really want something is if you still want it after you leave the store. Delaying purchases by a day, a week, or a month can make a big difference. Instead of purchasing that item you feel you must have right then, place it back on the shelf. Go home and research the item—the quality of it based on consumer reviews, how long it will last, and if you can find it elsewhere for a better price. After you've waited and done your research, you will know whether the item is a great deal or not. I promise it will be worth the wait!

ACTION STEP: The next time you're shopping and run across something you really want, make yourself put it back on the shelf and wait a day before buying it. You might be surprised by the items that never cross your mind after you leave the store!

STOP BROWSING

One of the easiest ways to curb spending is to simply refrain from shopping. Shopping is a hobby for some, but spending money you don't have shouldn't be a pastime. How many times have you told a store clerk you were "just browsing," only to leave the shop with purchases you never intended to make? How many times have you bought things you never used? You might then feel guilty for both the purchase and because you haven't used the item you've spent money on. I know this feeling all too well.

To combat the temptation to buy things I don't really need, I stick to the few stores where I get our groceries and household supplies and make the rest of our purchases online. But even with online purchases, you must train yourself not to browse. If you find yourself logging on to your favorite deals site every day, you might have to take extreme measures and block that particular website from your browser (at least for a time!). Make a goal to visit online stores only when you actually need to buy something and not when you're bored and just killing time. While it can be helpful to receive sales alerts via e-mail newsletters, if they tempt you to buy items you don't need, unsubscribe from them!

ACTION STEP: If you don't do so already, begin making shopping lists before you go shopping. Make it a goal to stick to your list, and don't veer into other parts of the store where you might be tempted to purchase things not on your list. If shopping is your pastime of choice, brainstorm a new hobby that won't cost you so much money with so little reward.

GIVE YOURSELF MAD MONEY

It sounds counterintuitive, but Will and I have seen success in curbing spending by giving ourselves some free-for-all money to spend each month. Some people call this fun money while others call it mad money. The basic idea is that each spouse will have a small portion of the budget each month to spend however he or she wishes.

Setting aside fun money can help keep you from overspending because it gives you a boundary. Even a $5 splurge on a fancy coffee once a month can keep you from making unnecessary purchases. Together, we've decided for Will to get more fun money than I do. Why? I don't like spending money, but he is admittedly enticed by the latest gadget. A solution is to give him enough fun money to satisfy his spending tendencies without allowing him to go overboard. Right now that means Will gets about fifty percent more fun money than I do each month, and I'm fine with that—especially since some months I don't spend my allotment at all, so it accumulates!

ACTION STEP: Talk to your spouse about the concept of "mad money." Ask if he would be willing to add this to your budget so you can create boundaries for little splurges. Then decide together how much fun money you will give yourselves to spend each month.

BARTER

When I was a child, I was always intrigued by the way my favorite *Little House on the Prairie* characters bartered for food and goods when they were low on money. *Why don't we still barter today?* I would ask myself.

Fast-forward to my adulthood, and I've learned that it *is* still possible to barter. No, big chain stores won't let you barter for food, but you might be surprised by how many things you can barter for.

My friend Kelly is a graphic designer who has traded her services in return for free advertising. I've done this myself on my blog. My friend Brandi, a hairstylist, has bartered for chiropractic adjustments.

Do you have a skill that you can use to barter? Maybe you can tutor your accountant's children in exchange for tax preparation. Or maybe your friend can cut your grass if you bake and decorate a cake for her child's birthday party. The opportunities are limitless! Get creative, and don't be afraid to ask your friends and acquaintances if they are willing to barter with you.

ACTION STEP: Jot down any skills you have that others might need. Then make a list of people who might be willing to trade their skills and services in exchange for yours.

HACK YOUR OWN HAIRCUTS

When I was growing up, my mom cut my hair. I never went to a hair salon until well into my teen years. My younger sister and I look back and laugh at the big bangs our mom gave us in the 1980s and early 1990s, but, hey—we looked just like the other kids did back then! Those bangs were a trendy style during our childhood, and my mom saved money by cutting them herself.

Not only did my mom cut her three kids' hair, but she also cut my dad's and her own! She also colored her own hair using drugstore dyes and even permed it herself when curls were the rage of the day.

Today, you can learn to cut hair via YouTube tutorials. Investing in a good pair of scissors and clippers can go a long way—especially for boys and men whose hair doesn't require as much maintenance. No, you probably won't be as talented as a professional stylist at a posh salon, but you might do a better job than you think.

What if you simply *don't* have the motor skills for DIY hair cutting? I feel your pain. I don't either! There are still other ways to save on haircuts:

Choose discount salons. While haircuts at top-end salons can cost $30 to $45 for an adult (minimum!) and $20 for a child, you can get a haircut for less than $10 at chains like Great Clips, Supercuts, or Fantastic Sam's. Places like these are usually walk-ins, but if you find a stylist you love, call ahead to find out if he or she will be working when you want to get your hair cut. My mom has been frequenting Great Clips for many years now, and she almost always has the same stylist cut her hair. You can also find coupons for discount hair salons, making them even more affordable.

If these discount salons scare you, another way to save is to ask for an entry-level stylist at a more upscale salon. These stylists likely offer more affordable rates than the more seasoned ones.

Search for a local cosmetology school for supervised services. How do you think hair stylists learn to cut and style hair? With hands-on experience! You can help a student practice and save money in the process. Call your local cosmetology school to ask for rates, and I can almost guarantee you will be slashing the price of haircuts and other personal-care services. You might also be able to get a wax and your nails painted!

While it might feel a bit scary to have a student cut your hair, keep in mind that instructors are usually walking around and observing the students while they cut your hair, and sometimes students are even being graded. This isn't a guarantee that you won't get a bad cut, but more often than not it means you'll be paying less for a good experience.

Select low-maintenance cuts and styles. I don't know about you, but when I became a mom, the need for quick-and-easy hairstyles became a necessity. I no longer have hours to spend primping in front of the mirror (as my parents said I did in high school!).

Especially when I was a stay-at-home mom to an infant, a toddler, and a preschooler, easy styles were a must.

Low-maintenance cuts and styles will ensure you need less upkeep. Choose hairstyles that don't need to be trimmed every month. For example, long styles will mean you need fewer haircuts. And by choosing to air-dry your hair (which is possible if you are a stay-at-home mom who doesn't need to leave the house early), you can maintain a healthy mane without having to get dead ends cut off as regularly.

ACTION STEP: If you're open to cutting your own hair (and/or the hair of your husband and children), designate an hour this week to search for YouTube tutorials that will help you get started. If you don't think DIY haircuts are for you, spend that time researching discount salons and cosmetology schools in your area.

CANCEL SUBSCRIPTIONS

While auto shipments like Amazon Subscribe & Save and other subscriptions can sometimes save you money, they are often something you can cut from your budget. You might even be paying for things you don't really need anymore because you've had a long-term subscription.

ACTION STEP: Go through your bank statement and highlight any subscriptions you can cancel. Cancel them today!

SLASH YOUR PHONE BILL

I'm not going to tell you to give up your phone altogether; in today's culture, having a phone is almost a necessity—especially for emergencies. But you don't have to pay an astronomical phone bill. There are real, tangible steps you can take to lower it.

Cancel your home phone service. Many people have found that having a home phone line is an unnecessary expense that can easily be cut, especially if both you and your spouse have cell phones. Some worry that not having a home phone line will hinder emergency services from pinpointing your exact location, and while this can be a valid concern, the Federal Communications Commission reports that seventy percent of all 911 calls come from mobile phones.[1] To safeguard yourself in case of an emergency, tell the operator your location and cell phone number immediately (in case you get disconnected). Note that if you are living on a very low income, the government might subsidize your phone bill. Check into this option via your state's department of social services website.

Opt for a VoIP phone. VoIP or voice-over-Internet phones gained popularity in the early 2000s. These offer home phone service for a lower price than most long-distance plans, but they allow you to keep a line separate from your cell phone. An advantage of VoIPs is that you are able to make calls internationally for a fraction of the cost you would pay via other phone services. Our family has been using a VoIP from Ooma (ooma.com) since 2008. We secured it when they offered it for a one-time payment, and we haven't had a home phone bill since! Ooma now charges a minimal yearly fee, but the savings is still incredible.

Choose a low-cost cell phone company. Don't discount the smaller and lesser-known cell phone companies without first checking into them. Will and I use Straight Talk (straighttalk.com), which we purchase through Walmart. Another company that friends of mine rave about is Republic Wireless (republicwireless.com). Especially if you don't require much data, one of these phone services might be a perfect fit for your needs.

Use prepaid cell phones. If you don't make a ton of calls but need a phone for occasional use and emergencies, a prepaid cell phone can save you money. Note that the cost per minute can be more than contractional plans, though, so this solution is best for those who do not use their phones often.

Consider a basic flip phone without data. Not only are flip phones more affordable because you won't be paying for data, but they can also help safeguard your family from the lost time that smartphones can suck away from you when you don't even realize it.

Bundle your services. While I recommend cutting cable if you want to save money, if you feel you simply can't live without it or a home phone line, you might save by bundling your cable, Internet, and phone bill.

ACTION STEP: If you still have a home phone line, evaluate whether you really need it. If you do, research some VoIP providers to see if switching to one of these can save you money. Then research the various cell phone providers in your area and compare prices. Check into whether you can save money by changing cell phone carriers.

REUSE WHAT YOU CAN

When we were living on a low income, I was also attempting to transition our family to a more eco-friendly lifestyle. I found that green and frugal living can go hand in hand. Starting with cloth diapers, Will and I learned how to trade out other disposables in our home for reusables that would save us money in the long run.

While our family doesn't pretend to be disposable-free one hundred percent of the time, over the years we've saved hundreds of dollars by sometimes using cloth napkins instead of disposable napkins, using dish towels for spills and regular cleanup instead of paper towels, and investing in reusable snack and sandwich bags instead of ziplock bags.

> ACTION STEP: The next time you spill something in your home, use a dish towel to wipe up the spill instead of a paper towel. Invest in an affordable set of cloth napkins, and begin using these for just one meal per day. If you're really brave, move your way up to trying other reusables in your home and life!

USE CLOTH DIAPERS

When we had a baby and a toddler at the same time, we couldn't afford twice the number of disposable diapers. Enter cloth diapers. If someone had told me when I was a newlywed that I would be a cloth-diaper user, I would have laughed. But the truth is, cloth diapers really aren't bad at all—and they can save you big.

At this writing, I am using many of the same cloth diapers I used on my first child with my fourth! Modern cloth diapers come with an up-front investment, but they can pay for themselves many times over—especially if you use them for more than one child. We've now saved thousands of dollars by using cloth diapers and cloth wipes instead of disposables.

Using cloth diapers doesn't have to be all or nothing. Since I was in a busy season of writing this book during my fourth child's first year, I decided to be a part-time cloth-diapering mama. Our son wore cloth diapers at home, but I put him in disposables when we were running errands. With each disposable diaper costing anywhere from 10 to 25 cents each, even part-time cloth diapering can save you money.

If you can't afford the up-front costs of cloth diapering, check into a cloth-diaper grant or loan from The Rebecca Foundation (clothforall.com) or Giving Diapers, Giving Hope (givingdiapers givinghope.org). If you need help learning how to use cloth diapers, check out my comprehensive handbook *Confessions of a Cloth Diaper Convert* at clothdiaperconvert.com.

ACTION STEP: If you still have children in diapers, consider making the switch to cloth. Check into one of the above organizations if you cannot afford the up-front costs. If you can, purchase a handful of diapers and challenge yourself to try using cloth diapers for one month. Using them might be easier than you think, and you'll save your family a lot of money by doing so.

TURN OFF THE LIGHTS!

I can still hear my mama's voice: "Turn out the lights! You're going to run up the electric bill!" In actuality, turning out the lights when you leave a room doesn't save you a ton of noticeable money, but over time, any savings adds up.[2] Unless you live in a mansion, it takes minimal time to turn off the lights as you leave a room. It's also just a good habit to get into and to teach your children.

ACTION STEP: Talk to your spouse and children about the importance of turning out lights when you leave a room. Tell them you're hoping to save money, and this small gesture can help lower your electric bill in the long run.

WASH LAUNDRY IN COLD WATER

I can't remember who gave me the tip about washing clothes in cold water, but I'm so indebted to her. In the nearly thirteen years I've been married, I've washed almost all our laundry in cold water and saved money in the process!

If you wash on cold, you can be cutting the energy your washing machine uses by nearly ninety percent![3] It also ensures that you don't run out of hot water when it is time to take showers, and it helps preserve the life of your clothing and linens. Hot water does the most damage to clothing, so it's best to reserve hot water use for heavily soiled items. The only laundry I wash with hot water on a regular basis are our bed linens and cloth diapers.

If your clothing gets especially soiled with sweat or dirt, an alternative can be washing with warm water (which will be cheaper than washing on hot) and rinsing with cold water. Once the clothing is washed, there isn't much point in rinsing on hot since the laundry will already be clean. Use cold water as much as possible!

As an aside: try to always run full loads through the washing machine. You use about the same amount of energy regardless of load size, so it's better to stick with a full load.[4]

ACTION STEP: Start washing your laundry with cold water, and watch your energy bill decline! Try it for at least one month so you can compare bills and see what a difference it makes to wash on cold.

LINE-DRY CLOTHES

I spent the year after I graduated from college in Costa Rica. There, it was common for people to line-dry *all* their clothing. In fact, it was uncommon for most families to own a clothes dryer! With a hot climate, it didn't take too long for the clothing to dry.

I realize that not everyone lives in a climate conducive to quick line-drying, but most of us in the United States get at least a season or two each year when it's possible. (And those who live in the South, like I do, can line-dry almost year-round!)

Line-drying your clothing can save you money on your electric bill, and it also comes with the added bonus of sometimes helping remove stains from your clothing (the sun bleaches them!). Air-drying can also keep clothing from wearing out as quickly and doesn't shrink materials like the dryer sometimes can.

Before you begin line-drying your clothes, check your home-owners' association (HOA) rules to make sure it's allowed where you live. An alternative to line-drying is using a foldout drying rack inside your home.

It *will* take longer to dry your clothes on the line. While I line-dried all my clothes, towels, and bed linens when I lived in Costa Rica, I now use a combination of both my dryer and a drying rack. For example, I use the dryer for sheets, towels, and anything that would take a long time (or lots of space) to air-dry, but I use my drying rack for jeans, underwear, swimsuits, and most of my blouses. If your clothes feel stiff after you've line-dried them, you can always throw them in the dryer for just a few minutes on the fluff cycle.

When you do use your clothes dryer, make sure you clean the lint filter after every use. Not only does this help the dryer run more efficiently (saving you energy costs), but it also helps prevent dryer fires.

ACTION STEP: If you live in a neighborhood with an HOA, check the rules to determine if line-drying is allowed. If it is, invest in a retractable clothesline and try line-drying. If your subdivision forbids line-drying, purchase a folding drying rack and begin using it in your home.

COOK ENERGY EFFICIENT

In the next chapter, I will emphasize that eating at home as much as possible is key to reining in your food budget. But even the types of appliances you use to cook can save you money.

Ovens require more energy to run than smaller appliances. Also, the heat they emit triggers your air-conditioning unit to run harder to cool your home. Instead, opt for smaller appliances that won't run up your electric bill. Some of my favorite small appliances to use are a slow cooker, a toaster oven, and a pressure cooker. My family also enjoys using a small electric skillet and a waffle maker to make breakfast foods, and skillet meals on the stove top are also fast, easy, and efficient—my favorite type of dishes to cook!

ACTION STEP: Make a list of all the meals you make regularly for your family. Then go through the list and determine which of those meals can work with the use of smaller appliances instead of the oven. Make it a goal to use your oven one fewer time per week this month. Work toward using your oven only once per day or even once per week.

AVOID TRIGGERS

Every spender has at least one trigger. Common triggers include grocery shopping while hungry or shopping while stressed or fatigued. Or one particular store may tempt you to overspend.

When I was pregnant with our first child, I quickly became addicted to browsing Craigslist for discounted and secondhand baby clothes, gear, and especially Robeez—an expensive leather infant shoe brand that was popular at the time. Even after we had all we needed for our baby, I continued to browse the online classifieds site. When I realized how much of a temptation this was becoming for me, I had to stop looking. I also removed myself from Facebook buy/sell/trade groups because they only tempted me to purchase things we didn't need. Now, I only rejoin these groups or visit other second-hand shopping sites if I'm looking for something specific.

ACTION STEP: Spend a few minutes jotting down some of your triggers. If you're a saver by nature, you might not know these off the top of your head. Ask God to reveal them to you. Share your triggers list with your spouse or a trusted friend. Ask that person to help keep you accountable when it comes to avoiding your triggers.

SAVE FOR CHRISTMAS YEAR-ROUND

Will is a huge gift giver. It's his love language, so you'd better believe it would break his heart if we had to skip giving Christmas presents—especially to our children. To make sure we don't have a large bill around the holidays, we designate a portion of our monthly budget to Christmas gifts. We decide what we plan to spend, divide it by twelve, and then each month we stock away that amount in a special Christmas fund. You can do the same—and avoid going into debt during the holidays.

ACTION STEP: Speak to your spouse about the possibility of opening a special savings account for Christmas presents. If he is okay with it, open it today and begin designating a portion of your monthly budget to this new Christmas fund!

PRACTICE THE THREE GIFTS TRADITION AT CHRISTMAS

When our firstborn was a baby, some of our friends told us that they had a tradition of giving their children just three gifts at Christmas— something they wanted, something they needed, and something to foster spiritual growth. We loved this idea and began it that year. Our four children have never known a Christmas when they got anything more than those three gifts (plus stocking stuffers) from us. They don't feel deprived (and, I can assure you, grandparents and aunts and uncles still gift them plenty!), and it's a fun tradition for us. It also helps us not overspend!

The three gifts idea comes from the recognition of the three gifts the wise men gave to Jesus when they visited Him. We are able to talk about the significance of the biblical story with our children as they open their gifts.

The "something they want" gifts are usually easy ones to find. "Something they need" has taken on different forms over the years. One Christmas we gave our little girls new princess sheet sets. They needed new sheets, and the princess ones were cute and fun! But we've also included educational games as "need" gifts because they fulfill the need for learning aids. The gifts to foster spiritual growth have sometimes been a challenge, but they've always been worth it. We've given them new Bibles, devotional books, Christian children's magazine subscriptions, Bible story puzzles, and one time even a Melissa & Doug Noah's Ark toy.

ACTION STEP: Decide if the three gifts tradition would be something you can implement in your family. Begin to brainstorm ways to tell your family about this new tradition—and what gifts you will give to your children to fit these three categories this year. (Some people add a fourth gift, which you might want to consider as well: something to read.)

KEEP KIDS' BIRTHDAY PARTIES AFFORDABLE

When I was expecting our first daughter, thinking about throwing her birthday parties was the last thing on my mind. As my daughter's first birthday drew closer, however, I realized just how much I wanted to make her feel special.

Over the years we've learned how to throw fun birthday parties for our kids—without breaking the bank! Here are a few of my favorite ideas for making your child feel special without spending a fortune:

1. Use a free (or low-cost) venue, like your home or the park. Nearly every birthday party we've ever thrown has been at a park or our own home. Our town charges a fee for using park facilities, but the cost is still much cheaper than other venues.

2. Make your own cake or cupcakes. I spent hours crafting an elaborate princess cake for my oldest daughter's first birthday. I solicited the help of a couple of friends and made it into a really fun moms' day! A homemade cake doesn't have to be fancy, though. I grew up on cakes my mom made from Betty Crocker mixes. They were delicious, and I never once thought they were anything but exciting. Yes, those were the days before Pinterest, but your children care more about how a cake tastes than how it looks (and how much it costs!). Don't feel like you have to impress your guests with a fancy-schmancy cake. That's stress you don't need in your life.

3. Keep the food simple. Schedule your party for midmorning or late afternoon so your guests won't expect a meal. You can simply serve cake, ice cream, and a beverage (juice, lemonade, iced tea, or even just water).

4. Allow your guests to save money too. Tell your guests that gifts aren't necessary (our kids, for one, *don't* need more toys!). We will sometimes ask guests to bring a donation to a local charity instead of gifts.

5. Shop at bargain stores for paper products and decorations. Dollar Tree is my personal favorite!

6. Combine parties with a friend. Split the costs and enjoy celebrating together!

7. Keep activities low-key. One year our daughter's guests colored pictures of tea sets and princess crowns, ate cupcakes and drank juice, and spent the rest of the time playing with her toys.

8. Be creative with the favors—or forgo them altogether. Cheap toys and candy? Most parents don't like bringing that stuff home. If you still want to give something, try:

- balloons
- bubbles
- a box of raisins or pack of fruit snacks

One year we gave out tea cups (bought at a thrift store) that we used as flower pots. The little girls planted seeds in the cups during the party. The cups cost next to nothing and went perfect with our "Princess Tea Party" theme!

ACTION STEP: Begin thinking about which of these tips you can use when it comes time to plan your child's next birthday party. One easy thing you can do today is to call your community's parks and recreation department to ask if they charge residents to use local parks for parties. Find out the cost (if any), and begin planning your next party!

SAY GOOD-BYE TO THE JONESES

For those of us who grew up in the 1980s and 1990s, "keeping up with the Joneses" was a values system so ingrained in our culture that it was the default for many. My neighbor lives in a large home? That must mean I should too. The girl next door wears designer shoes? I must buy designer as well. The family across the street takes a trip to Disney World every summer? We must attain that.

From house size to cars to clothing to accessories and vacations and every category under the sun, the American Dream has morphed into keeping up with those around us. Instead of living within our means and practicing the discipline of contentment with what we have and how God has provided for us, we've depleted our savings accounts, dug ourselves into debt, and burdened our emotional and mental capacities with the stress that comes with keeping up with the Joneses.

If you want to stay home with your kids, you will inevitably have to make sacrifices. Keeping up with the Joneses might be one of them. But I will tell you that contentment with a little will lead to great gain (1 Timothy 6:6), and you won't regret staying home with your kids.

ACTION STEP: As you finish out this chapter, ask God to reveal to you ways you can curb spending in order to better steward your money and give your family enough breathing room for you to stay home with your kids. If you've ever been tempted to keep up with the Joneses, ask the Lord to help you cultivate contentment with what you already have.

Many people claim that it takes massive amounts of money to eat healthy. Our family lived on a low income for several years, and this period of our lives coincided with when I was learning about how to eat more healthfully. I spent many shopping trips staring longingly at the organic food section—knowing I couldn't afford those items. While I don't deny that the more money you pour into your grocery budget, the healthier the food you'll be able to buy, I'm here to share with you ways you *can* feed your family well on a budget. Yes, it might take a little extra work and creativity, but if you want to stay home with your kids *and* feed them healthfully, the following tips will help you do it.

MAKE MEAL PLANNING A HABIT

Confession time: when left to my own devices, I often fly by the seat of my pants. Planning ahead does not come easily to me—especially when it comes to matters of the home. I know I'm not alone in the temptation to wing dinner each night! But I've learned that forgoing meal planning can cause you stress, endanger your health, *and* hurt your budget.

Regular meal planning will help you spend less money—both at the supermarket and by curbing the temptation to eat out. When I operate out of a well-planned menu, I don't buy food items we don't need (and, thus, end up not using). Instead, I make every penny count because I'm only purchasing what I need to feed our family according to each week's plan. Not only this, but when I fail to plan meals, our family ends up going out to eat more often than usual. With it costing upward of $50 per meal when my family of six goes out to dinner, eating out can sabotage our food budget in no time.

Meal planning can be as simple as making a list of dinners on a notepad or kitchen chalkboard at the beginning of each week. It doesn't have to be fancy or elaborate. Check out my e-course on meal planning at whats4dinnerchallenge.com if you're stuck in a menu rut.

ACTION STEP: Begin meal planning this week! Check out the meal-planning worksheet in my free resources for this book at thehumbledhomemaker.com/sahm-book-freebies. Use the password *icanstayhomewithmykids*.

COOK FROM SCRATCH

When I was a new wife back in 2005, I had no clue how to cook—much less cook from scratch. In fact, I had all of three recipes in my repertoire: a spaghetti pizza pie, a chicken pot pie, and a taco pie. Needless to say, my husband tired of pie within our first week home from our honeymoon!

Fast-forward to 2008, when I was expecting our first child and our finances began getting tighter. I realized I needed to learn how to cook, and to cook from scratch in order to save us the most money.

I bought several cookbooks and started learning, little by little. I desperately wanted to feed my children healthy foods, but we didn't have a Whole Foods budget, and I wasn't going to sacrifice my dream of staying at home with my kids in order to do it.

Nine times out of ten it will be much more affordable to cook from scratch than to buy premade, processed convenience foods from the store. But what if you don't know how to cook? Although I'm still far from being a gourmet chef or even an amazing cook, I learned to cook from scratch by simply following recipes. To this day, I almost always follow recipes when cooking. There is no shame in simply following directions!

If you lack cooking confidence, check out your local community colleges and/or community centers for cooking classes. If you have an Internet connection, you also have a plethora of online cooking schools at your fingertips. Also, don't shy away from asking an older woman from your church or neighborhood if she would be willing to help teach you the ropes of cooking. She might be delighted you asked! Our grandparents and parents learned domestic skills from the generations before them. I fear this passing down of skills is becoming a lost art. But it doesn't have to be!

You will probably find that staying home with your kids allows you more time for cooking from scratch. Yes, it is more time intensive to cook this way, but if you are home, you will have more margin to do so—and save your family money in the process.

ACTION STEP: Pick out a favorite cookbook and begin cooking through the recipes. Some of my favorites include the *Trim Healthy Mama* cookbooks and the *Good Cheap Eats* cookbooks. Check your local listings for affordable cooking classes, or search online to find one. Consider signing up for one of these classes to gain more confidence in the kitchen.

KEEP A PRICE BOOK

If you find yourself shopping at more than one store in order to get the best deals, it might be beneficial to keep a price book. I first learned this concept from my friend Anne Simpson, author of the e-book *Your Grocery Budget Toolbox*. A price book is a document that helps you track the prices for the foods you buy, listing the regular prices at each grocery store you frequent. This helps you quickly assess which supermarket has the best prices for your items. A price book can be any kind of notebook or spreadsheet or even a memo on your phone.

Keeping your price book will entail quite a bit of work, depending on how many stores you frequent. But the savings can really add up in the long run!

To start your price book, follow these basic steps:

1. Determine where you will keep your price book. A small notebook that you can keep in your purse or a note on your phone both work great.
2. Make a master grocery list in your price book. Include everything you ever buy on this list.
3. Set a date to visit all your local stores, and record how much each item on your list costs at each store.

Voilà! You have the basic shell of a price book. You will also want to record regular notes in your price book—like when stores have sales, which stores will price match, and stores' coupon policies. You will also want to update prices occasionally as they change. And don't forget to include online stores in your price book!

How does this help you shop? With the aid of a price book, you don't have to wonder if the items on your list are cheaper at another store. Your price book will show you the best place to purchase each item.

ACTION STEP: Begin making your price book. I have included the bones of a basic price book sheet with the downloadable bonuses for this book. Visit thehumbledhomemaker.com/sahm-book-freebies and use the password *icanstayhomewithmykids* to access this freebie. Use this, or make your own. Then set a date to begin visiting your local supermarkets and listing prices in your price book.

SHOP AT DISCOUNT STORES FOR GROCERIES

Here's a secret: I don't love shopping, period. While many women could spend hours on end shopping for clothes, jewelry, accessories, and even groceries, I would rather sit outside a store and read a book (and I did do this as a child when my mom, sister, and I would go shopping!).

But there is one type of store where I actually get at thrill out of shopping—and it's discount stores. In fact, I purchase more than ninety percent of my family's food at the popular discount chain ALDI. ALDI is a no-frills establishment with simple displays, few name brands, carts that patrons "rent" for a refundable quarter, and a counter where customers bag their own groceries with sacks from home. These cutbacks come with significant savings for the shopper.

I began frequenting ALDI during my newlywed days more than a decade ago, and it's still where I purchase most of our groceries. I even buy our toilet paper there, and it's not the thin, scratchy kind either! Other chains similar in price and style to ALDI include Save-A-Lot and WinCo. Even dollar stores usually include a small food section and are worth exploring.

Two other discount stores that sell some groceries are Big Lots and Ollie's. Both are closeout stores, meaning they buy deeply discounted merchandise from stores that are going out of business and pass on those savings to their customers. A drawback to shopping at closeout stores is that you never know what you'll find. Unlike ALDI, which stocks regular items, you're never guaranteed to find the same items again at Big Lots and Ollie's. If you find something you love, stock up because you may never see it again!

Discounts at bakery outlet stores are also worth noting. When I was a child, my mother purchased much of our bread, crackers, and other baked goods from a bakery that sold day-old and near-expiration goods that she could feed to us immediately or freeze.

ACTION STEP: Check out your local listings for ALDI, WinCo, Save-A-Lot, Big Lots, Ollie's, dollar stores, and other discount chains. Then set a date to visit these stores in field trip-like fashion. Go with pen and paper in hand (or take notes on your smart-phone), and record which items at these stores can make their way onto your grocery list—and save you money in the process.

SELECT SHOPPING DAYS WISELY

Not every store has the same sales cycle, but every store has one. For example, my local ALDI starts new sales each Wednesday. I get ALDI ads in the mail on Tuesdays, so seeing the upcoming sales helps me make my shopping lists. I also know I need to shop before each sale ends on Tuesdays if there is a sale item I need or want.

Before recycling sales ads, pay attention to when sales start and stop. You'll be kicking yourself if you miss something you needed that's on sale because you didn't take note of the sales dates. (Believe me, I've been there!)

Begin recording when your favorite items are on sale, and look for a pattern. For example, some items will go on sale every quarter at around the same time. If you can predict when items will go on sale again, you can estimate how much you need to purchase during a sale to stock up—and when you need to be ready to stalk the store circulars again for the items to go back on sale.

> **ACTION STEP:** Begin studying sales flyers as if you were studying for a big exam. Take note of sales in your price book so you can begin to predict when your favorite items will go on sale again.

SELECT SHOPPING TIMES WISELY

As we just discussed in "Select Shopping Days Wisely," paying attention to sales cycles can save you big. But there are actually specific *times* to shop—and to avoid shopping.

If possible, shop alone. If you're a stay-at-home mom, this can be nearly impossible, but if it's at all feasible, do it! When you shop with your children, they will be more likely to tempt you to buy treats and other things that aren't necessary. You can shop alone after your husband gets home from work or on the weekends. Some women find shopping first thing in the morning, right when stores open, to be beneficial—they are able to get in and out of the stores quickly before their husbands leave for their jobs.

Don't shop while hungry. If you're hungry, you will be more likely to buy more food! Eat a snack before you go.

Avoid crowded times. Shopping on Saturdays and Sundays can be especially frustrating because they are usually the most crowded times, and the selection will be more picked over. The right-after-work rush hour of between 5:00–6:00 p.m. can also be crowded.

> **ACTION STEP:** Pore over your calendar to determine the best day and time for you to shop for groceries.

USE ONLINE DISCOUNTS

The sky is the limit with how much money you can save by shopping online. Our parents didn't have this luxury, and I'm thankful for it since it saves me time as well as money! Money-saving apps can help you track down coupon codes, discover the store with the best prices, and even reimburse you just for shopping at certain locations.

At this writing, two popular apps for finding coupons are the Ibotta app and the Target app. Ebates is another site that lets you get rebates by shopping online. As well, Swagbucks.com is a search engine that lets you acquire points redeemable for both cash and gift cards. Since these apps often come and go, my biggest tip is to get real-time reviews on money-saving apps by signing up for my blog's newsletter at thehumbledhomemaker.com or by checking out my favorite money-management sites for moms, moneysavingmom.com and passionforsavings.com.

> **ACTION STEP:** Check out the Ibotta and Target apps, and download them to your phone. Check out ebates.com and sign up for swagbucks.com to start earning points. Also, check out the money-saving websites I noted above, and sign up for their newsletters.

BUY IN BULK

It's often (but not always) cheaper to purchase food and household items in bulk. Especially if you have a large family, purchasing a membership to a warehouse store like Costco, BJ's, or Sam's Club might be worth the expense. In fact, many families find that these memberships pay for themselves many times over!

Even when we were newlyweds, Will and I always kept a Sam's Club membership because we were able to get gas for our cars at the best rate in town. Now, buying in bulk helps our budget even more because we have four growing children!

A word of caution, though: not all bulk pricing is cheaper. Don't assume that the prices will be better just because you can buy in large quantities. Always calculate the price per ounce or per unit, and compare it to what you pay at discount or mainstream supermarkets. There might be times when it still is more affordable to purchase in smaller quantities at stores like ALDI or Kroger than to purchase in huge quantities at warehouse stores. Thankfully, most stores have made calculating these numbers easy for us, as they display the price per unit on the price signs. Just make sure you will use what you buy. If you have a small family, for example, it might not be worth it to buy bulk amounts of produce that could go bad (unless you intend to freeze it).

There are other ways to buy in bulk besides at warehouse stores. Amish stores will often include bulk items for sale, and I find it a fun cultural experience to visit these. I also do some of my family's shopping at the online health foods store Azure Standard (azurestandard.com). Azure offers mostly organic foods—the same types of items you would find at Whole Foods or Earth Fare, but for a more reasonable rate (especially when buying in bulk).

My favorite online store to purchase bulk meats from is Zaycon Fresh. Zaycon Fresh contracts with local farmers to sell fresh meats all over the United States. Our family has been buying chicken and shrimp from Zaycon for years, and the company is constantly adding new meat selections to their store. At this writing, Zaycon offers salmon, beef, pork, and turkey (including sausages and a variety of cuts) in addition to chicken and shrimp. I purchase chicken in forty-pound boxes from Zaycon about twice per year, and I purchase twenty-pound boxes of shrimp. You can check out Zaycon Fresh here: zayconfresh.com/refer/thehumbledhomemaker.

One last way to consider buying in bulk: use your tax return. As my family has gotten more into healthy living, we've realized the importance of buying quality meats (when and if possible). Antibiotic-free, free-range chicken and grass-fed beef will always be more expensive than grocery store meats, and if your budget will only allow for meat from the supermarket, do not feel guilty!

We do the best with what we have. But if you do have a little extra money at tax season, for example, consider investing it in quality meat in bulk. My friend Diana, a blogger at myhumblekitchen.com, purchases an entire cow's worth of beef for her family with her tax return each year.

Another benefit of buying in bulk is that it saves you time. You won't need to visit the store as frequently if you buy in bulk.

ACTION STEP: Check your local listings for warehouse stores. Inquire whether you can check out these stores without a membership; some will give free trial days, while others do not require a membership to browse. Just as you did with discount stores, set a date to explore these stores and record what they offer and at what prices. This is the best way to determine whether a warehouse store membership is a good investment for your family. Check out Azure Standard and Zaycon Fresh online to see if they deliver to your area.

CONSIDER COUPONING

I want to start this tip with a disclaimer: I don't use coupons much at all. At one time I dabbled in couponing, but I found that it didn't fit my family's lifestyle or food choices. Our children all have food allergies, and we eat a mostly whole foods diet. Coupons for the foods we eat are not as readily available. I also found that the time investment to coupon enough to save a significant amount of money would serve me better learning how to create more income in a way that better matched my gifts (more on that in the chapter "Create More Income"!).

Although I don't personally use many coupons, I realize there is real savings to be found in them. Here are some quick tips from my mother—the coupon queen of my family:

- Keep coupons organized by item type or alphabetically in a binder or coupon folder. Place the coupons with upcoming expiration dates closer to the front so you see them.
- Reserve coupons for double and triple days if your grocer offers these. This maximizes the coupon's value!
- Stack manufacturer coupons with store coupons to save even more.
- Check the Sunday circulars for coupons, but also check out printable coupons at websites like moneysavingmom.com and passionforsavings.com.

ACTION STEP: If you've been using coupons but haven't organized them, invest in a binder and coupon folder and begin arranging them in alphabetical order and by date so you can better find them when you need them. Also, check out passionforsavings.com and moneysavingmom.com to discover new coupons this week.

TRY ONCE-A-MONTH SHOPPING

When my children were little, I went through a season when I shopped only once per month. I knew I had a limited monthly grocery budget, and shopping infrequently helped me keep it in check. Each shopping day was lengthy, but then I basically didn't have to shop for the rest of the month! Here's how to make it work:

Pick a day when you can spend the entire day shopping. While Saturdays can be the most crowded shopping day, you might have to choose this day for once-a-month shopping because you will want to do this without your children if at all possible. A great alternative would be to swap childcare with another friend who wants to do once-a-month shopping. If that is an option for you, it's better to choose a midweek shopping day.

Start early. This shopping trip will be tiring. You will most likely be visiting several different stores—supermarket chains, discount stores, and warehouse clubs. Start as soon as the first store opens.

Plan a slow-cooker dinner for your once-a-month shopping trip. Once you get home from this shopping venture, you will be worn out. With a month's supply of groceries to unload, the last thing you will want to do is cook! Having dinner ready in a slow cooker will save your sanity.

Stock up on frozen produce and meats you can freeze. The most common question I get about once-a-month shopping is how to keep the produce from going bad. Simple: we eat frozen produce. Start the month with fresh produce, and opt for fruits and vegetables that stay fresh longer—like apples and carrots. When you've eaten the fresh produce, pull out the frozen produce to consume. You can always opt for canned produce as well, although it will have much less nutritional value than fresh and frozen produce.

Don't forget household goods. You will also want to stock up on cleaning supplies, toiletries, and so forth. The last thing you want to do is run out of toilet paper before the month is over!

ACTION STEP: Next month, try a once-a-month shopping trip and see how much money you can save.

MAKE FREEZER MEALS

Cooking and freezing meals ahead of time can help ensure you always have meals ready to go—and don't have to make last-minute runs to the supermarket, which will eat away at your grocery budget. On busy weeks or even seasons when your margin for meal planning is limited, freezer cooking can keep you from overspending.

I have some friends who make freezer meals a regular part of their homemaking routine. I only occasionally do so. When I buy meat in bulk (see "Buy in Bulk" on page 77), for example, I kill two birds with one stone by making the meat into meals as I am dividing it up and packaging it. My favorite types of freezer meals are no-cook slow cooker freezer meals. With these, you simply put all the raw ingredients that would go into a slow cooker in a freezer bag. When you're ready to cook the meal, simply pull the bag out of the freezer and put its contents into your slow cooker!

Some freezer meals have to be thawed slightly or even overnight before you can cook them. This is why I prefer slow cooker freezer meals—I can put them into the slow cooker without having to worry about thawing them the night before.

Here are some resources for freezer cooking to get you started:

- Once A Month Meals: onceamonthmeals.com
- My Freeze Easy: myfreezeasy.com

- New Leaf Wellness: newleafwellness.biz
- My freezer cooking resources page: thehumbledhomemaker
  .com/?s=freezer+cooking+

One of the downloadable bonuses for this book is a freezer cooking cheat sheet, which gives you the life span of how long certain foods can last in the freezer. Access it at thehumbledhomemaker.com/sahm-book-freebies and use the password *icanstayhomewithmykids*.

> **ACTION STEP:** Check out the websites above and plan to try freezer cooking sometime within the next month. Take it one step at a time—choose just one recipe, and start from there. My recommendation is to start with a slow cooker freezer meal.

EAT SIMPLY

When Will and I first married, I thought I had to slave over a hot oven every night and regularly try out fancy gourmet recipes to impress my new husband. Once we started adding kids to the mix and saw our budget shrink during the economic recession, I quickly learned that we had to eat meals made with fewer ingredients in order to survive—and not just financially either. Because I was still a novice in the kitchen, I found cooking nearly impossible with a baby nestled in one elbow and a toddler wrapped around my ankles.

I learned that meals don't have to take long to prepare or include expensive ingredients to be healthy. In fact, when it came to our health and our grocery budget, it soon became apparent that less can be more. Fewer ingredients meant less money spent at the supermarket. And shorter cooking time meant more time spent with my family.

The following simple items can form the basis of a nutritious meal plan. Anyone can purchase the same basic foods to plan simple meals. These foods are cheap but healthy.

Here are some examples of meals that can be made with simple ingredients:

Breakfasts:

- scrambled, fried, or boiled eggs with toast and fruit
- omelet with cheese and seasonal vegetables
- oatmeal and fruit

- homemade yogurt with homemade granola or fruit
- homemade French toast stuffed with bananas and smothered in peanut butter
- breakfast quesadillas or burritos (Spread a thin layer of butter on a tortilla, sprinkle with cinnamon and sugar, fold up, and bake or fry. A healthier, more satisfying version can be made by layering a tortilla with shredded cheese, scrambled eggs, and vegetables. Roll and eat like a burrito, or fold and cook like a quesadilla.)
- homemade smoothies with fruit and water or milk with just a hint of spinach or other greens
- alternative breakfasts, like rice and beans with sautéed veggies (While living in Costa Rica in my early twenties, I learned that rice and beans are typical for breakfasts in Latin America! You can even take day-old rice-and-bean dishes, spoon them into a homemade cornmeal dough, and cook them like empanadas.)

Lunches or Dinners:

- peanut butter and banana sandwiches
- tuna or salmon melts
- tuna or salmon salad or sandwiches
- tomato sandwiches
- salmon or tuna patties
- egg salad or egg salad sandwiches

- crustless quiche (using cheese to form the "crust")
- rice-and-bean dishes
- bean burritos
- bean tacos
- veggie, bean, or cheese quesadillas
- boiled eggs and fruit
- loaded baked potatoes or loaded sweet potatoes
- garden salads with beans, cheese, and tuna or salmon
- thin crust "pizzas" made with tortillas as the crust
- veggie mini "pizzas" made with eggplant or zucchini slices as the crust
- squash or zucchini boats
- tomato soup with grilled cheese sandwiches
- sweet potato soup
- tuna or salmon chowder
- lentil soup
- black bean soup

Snacks:

- apples and peanut butter
- apples or oranges and cheese slices
- carrot and celery sticks and peanut butter
- bananas and peanut butter
- homemade yogurt and berries

- homemade fruit smoothies
- fruit salad
- homemade peanut butter smoothie
- cheese sticks
- hard-boiled eggs
- homemade Chex Mix

Desserts:

- black bean brownies
- three-ingredient peanut butter cookies (Combine 1 cup of sugar, 1 cup of peanut butter, and 1 egg. Bake at 350 degrees for 6 to 8 minutes.)
- cereal treat bars
- homemade Rice Krispies treats
- homemade Chex "Muddy Buddies"
- rice pudding

Yes, these suggestions are incredibly simple, but when you are trying to make ends meet on a set income, choosing to add simple, healthful meals to your menu plan will make your dollars stretch.

ACTION STEP: Begin adding some of the above simple meals and snacks to your menu this week.

EAT IN SEASON

One way to save money on fresh produce is to buy what's in season. Produce that is in season and grown locally often costs less than produce that has to be imported from elsewhere. For example, you might eat more soups with winter squashes and greens during the colder weather months but more salads with fresh peppers, tomatoes, cucumbers, and carrots during spring and summer.

Check out your local farmers' markets for potentially deeper discounts on in-season produce. That said, farmers' markets aren't always more affordable. It really depends on the area in which you live. There is a farmers' market near my home with astronomical prices because it is located in an affluent suburb, but just a few miles north, I found another market with better prices because it pulls from clientele with a more moderate income level.

ACTION STEP: Check out sustainabletable.org/seasonalfoodguide to learn when certain foods come in season. Find your closest farmers' market via localharvest.org/farmers-markets.

COOK CASSEROLES AND SOUPS

My husband loves nothing more than sinking his teeth into a large cut of meat. If I had my way, I would eat a plate filled with grilled wild salmon every night. But eating this way is expensive! Your meals will stretch further by incorporating casseroles and soups into your menus. Both use ground or shredded meats, and a little goes a long way. This doesn't mean you have to eat casseroles or soups every night, but including these in your meal plans just once or twice a week can make a difference.

ACTION STEP: Make a list of your favorite casseroles and soups. Add one of each to your upcoming weekly meal plans.

BUY WHOLE CHICKENS

One of my favorite ways to stretch a meal is to cook a whole chicken in a slow cooker. You can serve a whole roasted chicken as the main dish for dinner, or you can easily shred the meat and stretch it to make:

- enchilada, quesadilla, taco, burrito, or empanada stuffing
- soups
- casseroles
- sandwiches

Pulled pork and roasted or ground beef can be stretched in similar ways.

You can then use the bones from cooked meats to make homemade stocks to be used in soups or stews. While convenient, boxed broths can be both pricey and unhealthy when you begin to tally the preservatives that many brands include.

ACTION STEP: This month, try roasting one whole chicken each week. Experiment with different ways to stretch the meat into several meals.

CHOOSE CHEAPER CUTS OF MEAT

We've already discussed the beauty of stretching a whole chicken to make several meals, but if you're trying to get the best bang for your buck when it comes to meat in general, there are certain cuts of meat to choose. While it's always more affordable to go meatless, that's not always a realistic option—especially if you're married to a carnivore like I am!

Bone-in meats are almost always more affordable than boneless cuts. Some ground meats like ground beef will be cheaper than steaks, for example (a lot cheaper!). Dark-meat poultry, like chicken thighs, will also sell for a better price than white breast meat.

ACTION STEP: Plan your meals around cheaper cuts of meat. You don't have to go meatless to save money; try opting for bone-in chicken instead of boneless, ground beef instead of steak, and darker cuts of poultry instead of white meat.

DRINK WATER

It's a simple tip that can save you so much money: drink water. No, it's not completely free, since you probably have a water bill, but water is significantly cheaper than other beverage options. Soft drinks, juice, and adult beverages can add up—plus, none of these is as healthy for you as water.

I grew up drinking soft drinks from a young age. In the 1980s and 1990s, our culture was not as aware of the health implications resulting from constant soft drink consumption as we are now. I gave up soft drinks cold turkey when I was eighteen and a freshman in college. I will never forget standing at the drink dispenser in my university's cafeteria and having a light-bulb moment when I realized that I didn't even particularly enjoy soft drinks; I was drinking them out of habit. I decided to opt for water that day, and it has been my beverage of choice ever since (more than half my life at this writing!).

My children have grown up drinking water as the norm, so it's their beverage of choice too. None of my four children has ever tasted soft drinks, and by the time this book publishes, my oldest will be close to ten years old.

ACTION STEP: Begin switching to water for one meal per day. If you have older children accustomed to drinking soft drinks or juice, this might be a challenge at first. Have an honest conversation with your family about how you want to save money and improve your (and their) health by drinking more water. After you've successfully transitioned to water for one meal per day, move on to two meals and then snacks until water becomes your family's go-to beverage.

POTLUCK HOLIDAY MEALS

One easy way to save money on food during the holidays is to choose to gather with family or friends and share a potluck meal. I used to stress over the fact that we couldn't afford to invite other families over to eat often—until one day I realized that we *could* if we asked them to help contribute to the meal. Our loved ones have been happy to do this, and I regret the fellowship we lost with others during the time when I was afraid to ask anyone to potluck with us. Take it from someone who now enjoys potluck meals each holiday season: you won't regret asking others to contribute!

ACTION STEP: Do you enjoy hosting holiday meals but are nervous about the food bill? Start planning a potluck Thanksgiving or Christmas for this year!

DIY HOUSEHOLD PRODUCTS

When we were living on a low income and I was trying to do something, *anything*, to make staying at home with my kids possible, I turned toward DIYing as many home products as I could muster. The humorous thing is that I am not naturally crafty or good at DIY projects! I learned to do this as much as I could during a short period because I wanted to stay at home with my kids, and this was an easy way to save money.

What is even more advantageous about DIYing things is that you can later make and sell those same products and turn a profit in the process!

FOAMING HAND SOAP

If you're new to the natural-living scene, one of the ingredients in this recipe, Castile soap, might be unfamiliar. This nontoxic, highly concentrated soap might seem expensive at first glance, but it will last a very long time and will serve as an ingredient in many DIY cleaning recipes. I've ordered Castile soap online at Amazon.com and Vitacost.com, but most health stores and even Target carry it. This foaming hand soap recipe is so easy-peasy that you'll never buy it again!

Ingredients:
¼ part Castile soap
¾ part distilled water
2 to 3 drops essential oil of choice
   (optional, for scent only)
A foaming soap dispenser

To Make:
Combine soap and water in a bowl. Drop in the oils, and mix. Pour the solution into a foaming soap dispenser.

ACTION STEP: Purchase the ingredients for this soap, and try it for yourself!

AIR FRESHENER

I use this homemade air freshener to spray the insides of my trash cans every time I change out the bags. I also use it to spray the bathroom or kitchen when I need a quick way to eliminate stinky smells. It's so easy to make that you'll wonder how you ever lived without it.

Ingredients:
Water
2 to 3 drops essential oils of choice
A glass spray bottle

To Make:
Simply fill a glass spray bottle with water, and add several drops of your favorite essential oils or essential-oil blends. Shake slightly before using.

ACTION STEP: Gather the ingredients and make this homemade air freshener. Then cross store-bought air freshener off your shopping list forever!

TOILET BOWL CLEANER

This homemade toilet bowl cleaner uses two simple ingredients that you probably already have on hand.

Ingredients:
Baking soda
White vinegar

To Make:
Sprinkle some baking soda in the toilet bowl. Pour some white vinegar into the toilet, then swish and scrub with a toilet brush until the toilet is sparkling clean.

ACTION STEP: Don't wait until you run out of toilet bowl cleaner to try this. If you already have baking soda and white vinegar on hand, make this today.

SOFT SCRUB

Use this easy homemade soft scrub to clean your counters, sinks, the outside of your toilet, and the bathtub.

Ingredients:
3/4 cup baking soda
3 tablespoons Castile soap

Water
2 to 3 drops essential oils of choice
(optional, for scent only)

To Make:
Combine the baking soda and Castile soap in a bowl. Slowly add water until the mixture is the consistency of a smooth paste. Add several drops of your favorite antibacterial essential oil, such as tea tree, lavender, orange, peppermint, or lemon. Scoop some soft scrub onto a clean sponge, and start cleaning!

Tip: If you have stains on your bathtub, you can apply the soft scrub and let it sit for several hours before scrubbing and rinsing.

ACTION STEP: The next time your tub needs scrubbing, whip up a container of this homemade soft scrub and give it a try. You won't be sorry!

TILE OR LINOLEUM FLOOR CLEANER

We have three bathrooms in our home, and two have tile flooring while the third has linoleum. Thankfully, this easy homemade floor cleaner will take care of both—with two ingredients, no less!

Ingredients:	To Make:
White vinegar	Combine equal parts vinegar and water, and
Water	get mopping! For tough stains, try sprinkling a
Baking soda	generous amount of baking soda onto the stain
(optional)	or using the homemade soft scrub recipe to
	loosen set-in grime.

ACTION STEP: This week, clean your floors with this home-made tile and linoleum floor cleaner instead of what you normally use.

ALL-PURPOSE CLEANER

Several years ago my friend Lexie McNeill, creator of the natural skin-care company Lexie Naturals (lexienaturals.com), introduced me to this easy-peasy homemade all-purpose cleaner. It calls for leftover citrus peels, so I feel resourceful using it. Citrus fruits are at their lowest price in the winter, and I always have an abundance of peels then. Since I don't buy citrus fruits as frequently during the warmer weather months, I freeze the peels so I can make this recipe any time of the year. Lexie gave me permission to share this recipe with you. I hope you'll enjoy using it as much as I have!

Ingredients:
Citrus fruit peels (I typically use orange, but any citrus peels can work!)
Salt (amount varies depending on the amount of peels)
Vinegar (enough to cover the peels in the jar)
Distilled water
5 to 10 drops citrus essential oil (optional, for scent only)

To Make:
Fill a glass container with the citrus peels. Add salt to the peels. You only need enough salt to lightly cover the peels. Let them sit for 20 to 30 minutes (or longer). This will pull the oils from the peels and ultimately make your cleaning solution stronger. You only need enough salt to lightly cover the peels.

Next, fill the container with one-half water and one-half vinegar. Put a tight-fitting lid on the jar, and let the solution sit for two to three weeks. The longer it sits, the stronger the cleaner will become.

Strain the solution and fill a glass spray bottle with your home-made all-purpose cleaner. If you are using essential oils, add them at this time.

ACTION STEP: The next time your family is enjoying citrus fruit, don't throw out the peels. Instead, begin freezing the peels so you can make this homemade all-purpose cleaner. No need to thaw the peels before making it.

MIRROR OR WINDOW CLEANER

If you have young children at home, keeping your mirrors clean can be quite the challenge. I feel your pain, Mama! Those little hand-prints are the cutest things ever, but, if nothing else, you'll want a clean, fingerprint-free mirror before guests arrive. Thankfully, you can clean both your mirrors and your windows with just two ingredients.

Ingredients:
1 cup white vinegar
1 cup water
2 to 3 drops essential oils of choice (optional, for scent only)
A glass spray bottle

To Make:
Simply mix the vinegar and water in a glass spray bottle, and add essential oils if desired. Spray your mirrors or windows, and wipe clean with paper towels or newspaper. Yes, newspaper works great for wiping mirrors and windows!

ACTION STEP: Try this homemade mirror and window cleaner the next time you need to clean either.

DEODORANT

When our children were little, I began transitioning our family to living a more natural lifestyle. Part of this was switching our personal care items to nontoxic varieties, once I learned that many store-bought versions contain ingredients I didn't want to expose my children to.

But I faced a challenge early on: I couldn't *afford* the more natural versions. Instead, I began making my own. I made a variation of the following homemade deodorant recipe for years. To save on costs, omit the beeswax, and store it in a container in the refrigerator to keep it from melting.

The following recipe is from my friend Lexie of lexienaturals.com. She sells deodorant made from this recipe in her online store, but she generously allowed me to share her recipe.

Ingredients:

2 heaping tablespoons beeswax pellets (pellets are easier to measure)

1 tablespoon shea butter

5 tablespoons coconut oil

1/4 cup cornstarch (or arrowroot powder for very sensitive skin)

1/4 cup aluminum-free baking soda

10 to 15 drops tea tree essential oil

10 to 15 drops lavender essential oil

10 to 15 drops of other essential oils (optional, for scent only)

2 to 3 new or used deodorant tubes (cleaned and twisted all the way down)

To Make:

Melt the beeswax in a double boiler. Add the shea butter and coconut oil, and heat until just melted. Stir occasionally.

Remove from the heat, and add cornstarch and baking soda. Stir until the lumps are gone and the texture is smooth. Add the essential oils, and stir until well mixed.

Pour into old deodorant tubes, and let them sit a few hours before adding the tops. You will want to fill them until they seem to almost overflow because they will fall down a good bit once cooled. You can also fill the tubes halfway and let them sit 5 minutes before filling the rest of the way. This will ensure you fill them as full as possible.

Note: It can take a few weeks for your body to adjust to a more natural deodorant. As well, those with very sensitive skin may have a negative reaction to the baking soda.

ACTION STEP: Gather the ingredients and test out this home-made deodorant recipe.

Even though I know you may be reading this book because you want to be inspired with ways to save money to give your family more financial margin, I am not going to tell you to stop eating out, going on date nights, and taking your family on vacations.

Why?

Feeling restricted from doing something often sets people up for failure. One of my friends put it best when she said, "Be disciplined without being legalistic." Let's take eating out, for example. Discipline will allow you to give yourself a certain number of nights per month to eat out; legalism will say you can't eat out at all. Budgeting to enjoy a meal at a restaurant will give you something to look forward to, and it will also help you say yes to eating at home when you know you will be dining out soon.

Whether it be eating out, going on a date with your spouse, enjoying a family day with your kids, or taking a vacation, you don't have to spend a fortune. There are ways to enjoy these while spending less money in the process. We'll explore how in this chapter.

CONSIDER CABLE ALTERNATIVES

My husband and I paid for cable television during our newlywed years, and I regret that we poured so much money down the drain when I rarely watched TV and he liked only a handful of shows. Of course, back then we didn't have the plethora of entertainment options that we have at our fingertips now. We cut cable when we were living on a low income during the recession, and we've never looked back.

Cutting cable isn't a new suggestion for saving money, but I'm often asked about alternatives to cable. The good news is that there are many! The following are my top picks:

Netflix: Netflix is a subscription service that streams a wide variety of TV shows and movies for both kids and adults. You can view Netflix on television sets, computers, smartphones, and tablets as long as you have an Internet connection.

Hulu: Hulu is similar to Netflix, except that it streams current television shows the night after they air.

Amazon Prime: Prime members are able to stream a plethora of TV shows and movies. At this writing, low-income individuals can get it for a discounted rate.

Roku: This is a streaming device for your TV. You can pay for access to some channels, but others are free.

Sling TV: This is a live TV streaming service that offers options for watching sports.

To be even more frugal, stick to DVD rentals from somewhere like Redbox or borrow them from the library. I went without TV for a year when I was in college, and it cured me of my need to watch TV on a regular basis. It's been nearly twenty years since I've felt the need to veg out in front of the boob tube.

ACTION STEP: Cancel your cable subscription for one month, and see if you miss it. Fill in the gaps with one (or more) of the above alternatives to cable.

CHECK YOUR LIBRARY FOR FREE KIDS' ACTIVITIES

Libraries are much more than places to borrow books. Many public libraries also offer free educational and enrichment activities for children year-round! Beyond a summer reading program, our local library offers story times for babies, toddlers, and preschoolers, and they also offer after-school activities for older children—from Lego building to craft nights to movie marathons! Your local library might very well host free activity events as well.

ACTION STEP: Call your local public library (or check out their website) to see if it offers any free activities for kids. Mark the next event on your calendar, and take your kids.

EXPLORE LOCAL PARKS AND SPLASH PADS

It dawned on me a few years ago that our community is home to many parks that we had never visited. In fact, we live just miles from a state park with a lake, nature trails, and campsites—yet we lived in our town for eight years before we ever checked it out! Taking your kids to a new-to-them park will keep them occupied for hours. Throw together a picnic lunch, and you'll have entertained them for a fraction of what you would pay at some other venues.

Also, be on the lookout for parks that have splash pads during the summer months. These sprinkler systems are a safer alternative to pools, and I haven't met a kid who doesn't like cooling down in them in the heat of summer. Some parks might charge extra for entry to splash pads, but many are free.

ACTION STEP: Check your community's parks and recreation website for local parks, and visit stateparks.com/usa.html to find state parks that might make for a fun day trip. Search for splash pads in your area while you are at it.

TAKE ADVANTAGE OF FREE OR CHEAP SUMMER MOVIES

When our girls were preschoolers, we discovered that many theaters across the country offer free or cheap kids' movies during the summer. Some even throw in popcorn and a drink! The movies are usually a few years old, but watching them makes for a fun, affordable (or free!) summer outing with your kids. And if you live anywhere near the South (like I do), then you'll appreciate spending a few hours inside an air-conditioned theater to take refuge from the heat!

ACTION STEP: Search online for "free summer movies" or "cheap summer movies" near your town. If a theater near you offers this, print out the schedule and make some dates to attend the movies with your children.

SEEK OUT SCHOOL PLAYS

While a Broadway show might be cost prohibitive for many families (as is a trip to New York City!), your family can enjoy the arts right in your own community by seeking out school plays. Our family has enjoyed attending high school plays at the school where my husband taught for years as well as plays at our local community center. These aren't always cheap, but they are much more affordable than what you would pay for professional theater tickets—and attending them supports your local community.

ACTION STEP: Check your local listings for upcoming school plays. Make a date to see one with your husband or with your entire family.

CONNECT WITH YOUR SPOUSE ON THE CHEAP

I'm not going to lie: date nights are *expensive*. Dinner and a movie can now cost us up to $100—simply because we have to hire a babysitter to watch four children.

Or do we?

Have you ever considered trading childcare with a friend—*or* forgoing the dinner and a movie and having an intentional date night at home with Netflix and a big bowl of popcorn instead (after the kids are in bed, of course)? Date nights don't have to look like they do on television. With a little creativity, you can connect with your spouse on the cheap.

> ACTION STEP: Brainstorm date nights that are out of the dinner-and-a-movie box. Begin planning your next date night, with the intention of spending as little money as possible.

CHECK OUT FREE COMMUNITY CONCERTS

Many communities across the country offer free concerts for up-and-coming bands. Our town hosts these outdoors in the summer. Coffee shops are another good place to find free concerts and open-mic nights. These make great, cost-effective date nights!

ACTION STEP: Instead of going out to eat for your next date night, check your local listings for any upcoming free concerts. Trade childcare with a friend, and attend the concert for an affordable date night.

BUY A MEMBERSHIP

The larger the family, the more cost prohibitive activities can become. Our third child is five years old, so we are paying a full child's admission for three children—knowing our fourth won't be free for long!

Sometimes it makes more financial sense to buy a membership to certain venues. When our girls were younger, we used my husband's teacher discount to buy a membership to a local children's museum. This gave us a year's admission for what we would have paid for two visits!

We recently purchased a membership to our state's zoo. Admission costs our family $60 per zoo visit, but we were able to upgrade to a yearlong pass for just $20 more. Now we can visit the zoo at any time this year, and we also have free or discounted passes to almost every other zoo in the United States. My husband and I calculated that this was worth it—even if we only visit one other time this year.

If you invest in a membership, just be sure to use it. A good deal like this can be wasteful if you live too far away to use the membership enough to make up for the cost.

ACTION STEP: If you have any museums, zoos, or amusement parks nearby, check into the cost of a membership. It might give you more affordable entertainment options for your family.

PLAN AHEAD WHEN EATING OUT

I didn't date much before getting married, but I always giggle when I look back to one blind date I had in college. Nervous to go out alone with a stranger, a friend and I chose to go on a double date. I don't think the poor guy I was with had ever been on a date. When we got to the steak house, he broke out in a sweat when he looked at the menu and started commenting under his breath, "Man, this place is pricey." He loosened his tie a bit as his face reddened. "Oh boy—I don't know if I have enough money for this."

Feeling sorry for him, I ordered a $3 cup of potato soup.

We were all naive when we entered that restaurant, and although that memory still makes me laugh, I can't help but think about how many times grown adults choose an eating establishment without first thinking of how expensive the menu options will be.

Just like planning your meals at home, planning ahead before eating out can save you money at restaurants. While it's fun to try out new venues now and then, our family mainly sticks to eating at a handful of restaurants where we know going in that we won't be spending an arm and a leg on dinner.

Requesting takeout menus to keep at home can also help you prepare before going out to eat; not only will it save you time in selecting your entrée once you arrive, but it will also help you plan to stick within your budget by choosing menu items that are not too expensive.

If you do want to try a new restaurant, check to see if they offer an online menu. This can also help you decide if you can afford the restaurant before even stepping foot inside.

ACTION STEP: Visit the websites of some of your favorite restaurants. Print out their menus to have on hand for the next time your family is going out to eat there. Stick the menus in your homemaking binder or another place where you will be able to access them easily and often.

LOOK FOR "KIDS EAT FREE" NIGHTS

There are hundreds of restaurants that offer "Kids Eat Free" nights. In fact, you might be able to locate a restaurant for most nights of the week! Keep a running list of these restaurants, organized by the night kids can eat for free, and plan your eating-out nights around where you won't have to pay for the kids.

ACTION STEP: Search online to find the "Kids Eat Free" nights in your area. Keep a list of these via your free printable Kids Eat Free sheet that came with the downloadable bonus content for this book at thehumbledhomemaker.com/sahm-book-freebies. Use the password *icanstayhomewithmykids*.

SHARE MEALS (OR REQUEST A TO-GO BOX)

Most restaurants will allow people to share entrées. It is sometimes more cost effective to split a large meal than to purchase two smaller ones. And don't assume that children's portions are cheaper. It might be more affordable to purchase an adult entrée to split between two or more children. Also, let your kids eat off your plates, or share plates as long as possible. Kids' appetites are much smaller than adults'. Just tell your server you are sharing, and request that they bring an extra plate.

Restaurant portion sizes are notoriously large in the United States. If you can't finish your entire meal, don't leave it on the plate: request a to-go box!

ACTION STEP: The next time you're eating out, select a large meal that you and your spouse (or your children) can share. Or take home leftovers to eat for lunch the next day.

AVOID PEAK SEASONS

When booking your vacation, stay aware of peak seasons, and try to avoid them. That might mean that you take a vacation to the beach when it's too chilly to get in the water—but you will still be able to enjoy the seaside views. It might also mean that, instead of a winter ski trip, you visit the mountains in the summer. There will still be plenty to do, but you will pay a fraction of the price for lodging. At this writing, our family is planning a summertime mountain retreat that is going to cost us one-third what it would cost us if we were to go during ski season.

ACTION STEP: If you are able to take a family vacation this year, plan it for the off-season of your desired location. You will spend a lot less money but still make family memories that will last for years to come.

FIND MORE AFFORDABLE ALTERNATIVES TO HOTELS

While traveling, lodging can be expensive. Instead of staying at a hotel, check into whether one of the following offers a more affordable place to stay:

Airbnb.com: Individuals and families rent out their homes, apartments, or even individual rooms via this increasingly popular website. The rates are usually much more affordable than hotels.

HomeAway.com: HomeAway is similar to Airbnb.

VRBO.com: VRBO is also like Airbnb and HomeAway, but the rates are usually slightly higher. Some listings are on all three sites, so cross-check them for the best rates!

Camping: If you don't care as much about comfort, you can always pack a tent and spend vacation time at a campground. This will be your cheapest bet for lodging. Or opt to take a camping vacation. Some of my favorite childhood memories are of the camping trips I took with my family.

If you must use a hotel because one of the above isn't available (or doesn't suit your fancy), check out the following websites for hotel savings:

Trivago.com
Hotels.com

Booking.com
Priceline.com
Groupongetaways.com
Orbitz.com
Kayak.com
Hoteltonight.com

Many of these sites also work for finding affordable airfare and car rentals!

ACTION STEP: Don't just book a hotel for your next family vacation. Explore the above offerings to discover more affordable lodging.

SHOP SECONDHAND AND SALES

When you're trying to make ends meet enough to stay home with your kids, you have to learn how to cut corners in any way possible. But you, your spouse, and your children can't live on bread alone: you have to wear clothing and have something to sleep, sit, and eat on while at home. There is perhaps no easier way to add money back into your budget than by choosing to shop sales and secondhand when it comes to these items. I grew up in a frugal family, so I've never had qualms about buying used items. But I now realize that not everyone is accustomed to shopping secondhand. This section of the book will tell you just how to do it—and not look shabby (or sit on dilapidated furniture) in the process.

SHOP AROUND

When purchasing high-priced items, like furniture, it pays to shop around. While there are merits in customer loyalty, especially for local businesses, if you are pinching your pennies, you need to be willing to shop at more than one location. You might be surprised to find that two stores will offer the same item for different prices. This is the method we used when shopping for our first brand-new home furnishings (after we had been married for more than a decade!). We scored some major deals because we chose to research prices at more than one store.

ACTION STEP: The next time you're making a major purchase, check the selection and prices at more than one store. You won't be sorry!

CHECK OUT CONSIGNMENT SALES AND STORES

When I was expecting our first daughter, I discovered children's consignment sales, which later led me to a whole world of consignment shopping. Consignment shopping is a step up from both yard sales and thrift stores. The sellers of the used items go through a third party to sell their items. In return for providing the sales venue and advertising, the third party—the consignment sale or shop owner—takes a percentage of the earnings. An advantage to buying on consignment is that the items are often in better condition than what a buyer would find at a yard sale or in a thrift store. A disadvantage is that the items are usually priced higher since a third-party seller is involved.

Where I live there are several seasonal children's and women's consignment sales that pop up a couple times per year. The children's sales offer clothing, shoes, toys, books, school uniforms, baby gear, and more. The women's sales offer clothing, jewelry, accessories, shoes, handbags, and even some home decor. Most sales have strict quality control, making the inventory much more desirable. I enjoy shopping at these sales because they are short-lived—usually lasting only a few days to a week each—so they are not there long enough to tempt me to browse frequently (which is often the cause of spending more money than necessary). The sales in my area also

129

offer half-price days near the end of the sales, which gives an even greater incentive to buy.

In addition to temporary consignment sales, brick-and-mortar consignment shops can be found all over the country, selling anything from clothing to home decor and furniture year-round. Also, several online consignment businesses now allow consumers to shop second-hand from the convenience of home. Popular sites like Schoola.com, Swap.com, and Thredup.com boast that customers can save anywhere from fifty to ninety percent off retail prices, and they allow users to send in clothing, shoes, and accessories in a postage-paid bag and start earning money. One disadvantage of these stores is that they require you to spend money on shipping, or at least spend a certain amount before getting free shipping. But one advantage, as opposed to brick-and-mortar stores, is that their inventory is usually much larger.

ACTION STEP: Browse your local listings for consignment shops. Make a date to go check them out the next time you need something they offer—usually clothing or furniture.

TRY THRIFT STORES

My paternal grandmother began thrifting more than fifty years ago, when my father was a preteen. Then it was a hobby for her. When my grandfather left her in the mid-1970s with two of their five children still at home, she turned thrifting into an income stream. For the next twenty-five years until her death, my grandmother fully supported herself by buying and reselling high-end items at thrift stores and yard sales.

Having inherited the thrifting knack from his mother, my dad is now a thrift-shopping expert. When he retired a few years ago from his career as a hospital administrator, he took his hobby to a whole new level and began shopping at our local Goodwill and Habitat for Humanity stores twice per week.

While thrift stores have gotten a bad reputation for being smelly, dirty, and simply undesirable, that is not true in many cases. My father has found top-brand clothing, shoes, handbags, jewelry, china, and more on his shopping trips. He now shops with the aid of his smartphone, which can help him sift through brand names, but he will still occasionally come home with a buried treasure that he had no idea he was snagging.

Try these thrift-store shopping tips:

- **Go early and go often.** Inventory is constantly changing. Those who arrive when the stores open and stop by frequently will find the best deals.
- **Shop in affluent areas.** Stores in higher income areas are more likely to receive higher-end donations.
- **Clean items before you use them.** This is especially important for clothing, but you will also want to wipe down any items that you buy at a thrift store.
- **Inspect before buying.** This is a given with any kind of secondhand shopping. Quality is not guaranteed. Look for any signs of wear and tear before you put down any cash.
- **Ask about return policies.** You might be surprised that some thrift stores do allow returns, but not all do. It's always best to know the policies up front before you get stuck with items that you realize aren't up to par once you get them home.

ACTION STEP: This weekend check out some of the thrift stores in your area. You might be pleasantly surprised to find that they aren't as bad as their stereotype!

CHECK OUT YARD SALES

If you're looking for the lowest prices possible, this will be your secondhand shopping method of choice. Yard sale shopping will be more time consuming than other shopping methods because most people hold sales on the weekends and only during warmer-weather months. You will also have to find new sales each week instead of being able to frequent the same brick-and-mortar secondhand shops.

Because most sellers simply want to get rid of things, you will be able to negotiate more at yard sales than at any other secondhand shopping venue. One downside to yard sale shopping can be that the quality at some sales may be extremely low. It is also highly unlikely that you will ever be able to return an item to a seller's home, making yard sale shopping risky. Some sales can be hit-or-miss, but by employing some smart shopping strategies, you can save big.

While there is no limit to what you can find at yard sales, there are several items that usually sell the best and are higher quality. Baby items, furniture, and toys are some of the best yard sale finds because these do not wear out as fast as some other things. Our four children are still playing with Little People toys I scored at a yard sale when I was expecting our firstborn nearly a decade ago!

Follow these yard sale shopping tips:

- **Go early.** Many professional yard sale shoppers hit the road before 6:00 a.m.

- **Map out where you will go ahead of time.** Many sellers advertise via newspapers, Craigslist, and road signs ahead of time. It's best to have an idea of the sales you will hit up before you hit the road to make the most of your time.
- **Focus on as many group sales as possible.** Neighborhood, community, and church yard sales will give you access to more inventory and multiple families selling at the same time. Moving sales are also great ones to hit up because the sellers will be willing to negotiate at rock-bottom prices since they don't want to pack and move what doesn't sell.
- **Check out sales in affluent areas.** Just like with thrift shopping, you will be more likely to find high-end items at these sales.
- **Negotiate, negotiate, negotiate.** Don't be afraid to ask for lower than the asking price.
- **Bring cash.** Be prepared with small bills and plenty of coins in case the seller is not stocked with enough change.

ACTION STEP: When yard sale season starts in your community, take a Saturday and hit all the sales! You will never know if you like this secondhand shopping method until you give it a try.

SHOP CRAIGSLIST

Without a doubt, furniture has been our favorite find on Craigslist, but there are literally thousands of items you can score on the site. When we were expecting our first child, we purchased much of our baby gear on Craigslist, and we also found the townhouse we rented for four years on Craigslist. You can find gardening supplies, home decor, electronics, bicycles, scooters, wagons, motorcycles, vehicles, and even food on Craigslist! People do sell clothing as well, but I've personally had better luck finding clothing elsewhere.

As with everything, making a plan will help you save money in the long run. With that in mind, the following tips will get you started in making the most out of shopping on Craigslist:

- **Make a list of the items you need.** This will help you avoid impulse purchases!
- **Search the site.** Start checking your local Craigslist daily for the items on your list.
- **When you see an item you want, e-mail or call the seller and ask if the price is firm.** Unless the listing specifically says the price is firm, do not be afraid to negotiate! Most sellers will name a price with OBO, which stands for "or best offer."
- **Eye before you buy.** Don't commit to any purchases over the phone or via e-mail. Ask when you can see the items.

- **Take your spouse or a friend with you when you go to see and/or buy the items.** This is very important. Sadly, there are Craigslist scammers, and people have gotten themselves into some dangerous situations. Meet in a public place, or take at least one person with you if you are going to the seller's home to look at a larger item. If you have a bad feeling about it, don't go.

- **Never pay money until you see the items.** Some scammers will ask for a deposit via electronic transfer or PayPal. This is a dead giveaway that the lister is a fraud.

- **If you see another item you like at the seller's home, ask if it's for sale!** When we went to someone's house to buy a bookshelf, we also found a cabinet that we bought and turned into a changing table.

- **Use your creativity to make the items your own.** To make furniture purchases match the other furnishings in our home, we've stained and painted our Craigslist finds.

- **Check items thoroughly before buying.** With furniture especially, be sure to check for scratches, bugs, and so forth. Never buy used mattresses.

- **With electronics and other battery-operated items, make sure they work before you buy.** Also, with all purchases, check for broken hardware and missing pieces.

- **Realize the risk.** It's highly unlikely that a Craigslist seller will accept a return and issue a refund. Once you take an item home, it's yours, so be sure you are one hundred percent satisfied with and confident in your purchase before dishing out any money.

ACTION STEP: The next time you're in need of something, check Craigslist before you buy new. The search function works very easily, and you'll be happy with the money you save!

SHOP FROM HOME

No, I'm actually not talking about online shopping here—but literally meeting your needs by discovering items already lurking in your own closets and other storage areas!

A few years ago I decided that my wardrobe needed a complete overhaul. I needed new clothes, but I didn't want to spend a lot of money. My friend Holly suggested that I have her fashionable cousin, Candace, come over one weekend and help me shop from my own closet by putting together stylish outfits from the pieces I already owned. I was floored at the many beautiful outfits we put together with clothing that was already hanging in my closet! Candace was tactful but truthful about what clothes I needed to ditch, and she gave me some amazing tips about pieces that I should wear together.

You can also "shop from home" with furniture, home decor, and toys for your children. I'm now convinced that anyone can save money by "shopping" from what they already own. A bonus? You can declutter and get rid of items you truly will never use in the process!

ACTION STEP: Set a date to "shop" from various areas of your home that you've been meaning to declutter. Begin with shopping from your own closet. You might be surprised at the outfits you can put together without ever spending a dime!

START A CLOTHING EXCHANGE

If you have unwanted clothing in your closet and wish you could make room for more but can't afford a new wardrobe, you might want to consider starting a clothing exchange with a group of friends. A clothing exchange can be as organized as you want to make it. It can be an event held among a small group of friends, or you can open it up to your entire church or community organization. I have only participated in women's clothing exchanges, but I have heard of others forming exchanges for children's clothing, toys, and gear as well. The beauty of an exchange is that it allows participants to rid their homes of unneeded items while snagging what they do need—for free!

ACTION STEP: Brainstorm ways you can start a clothing (or gear) exchange. Solicit help from a group of friends, find a location (a home can easily work!), determine participant requirements (will they need to donate in order to take?), and decide what to do with leftover items (donating to a women's shelter is one option).

ACCEPT HAND-ME-DOWNS

When I was a kid, even though my parents could afford new clothing, we still wore plenty of hand-me-downs. My parents refused to pay full price for anything, and when friends, relatives, or neighbors offered my parents a bag of their child's outgrown clothing, they accepted it with no qualms. If someone offers you free clothing and you need it, there should be no shame in accepting it. Even as a woman in my mid-thirties, I still wear hand-me-down clothing.

If you're already overflowing with clothes and don't need anymore, though, it's okay to politely say no when someone offers you hand-me-downs. I struggled with saying no for years, and I ended up with more children's clothing than I could fit in our townhouse. I couldn't keep up with the laundry because I had so many clothes to wash. Alternately, you can accept hand-me-downs and simply pass down to others what you and your family cannot use yourselves.

ACTION STEP: The next time someone offers you a bag of hand-me-downs for your children (or even for you!), accept it. If the clothing items don't work for your family, hand them down to someone else or donate them.

CLEAR THE CLEARANCE RACKS

When I was a child, my parents taught me to head straight for the back of a store any time we went shopping. By the time I was a teenager and started shopping on my own, this practice had become a habit. To this day, I rarely ever glance in the direction of the full-priced items at the front of a store, especially when shopping for clothing. Instead, I head straight for the clearance racks.

While most stores have a small clearance section year-round, the best time to shop clearance clothing is at the end of each season. At stores like Kohl's and Target, I've been able to find clothing for my children at up to ninety percent off retail price! The key is to be willing to shop out of season. That means I will shop for fall and winter clothing at the beginning of spring and for spring and summer clothing at the beginning of winter. Stores needs to clear out inventory to make room for new items, so they are willing to slash tags to rock-bottom prices. In fact, clearance prices are often more affordable than consignment prices because the seller, the store, is more invested in moving inventory than in turning a profit. Some families have even created side businesses by buying clothing on clearance and reselling the items on eBay, consignment, or Craigslist.

Many stores also offer clearance sections on their websites. An upside to this is that you can shop from home and may not be as tempted to make unnecessary purchases as you might be if you ran across items in the store. A downside is that you will have to pay for shipping, but most stores provide free shipping if you spend a certain amount. I have found that I save both time and money by shopping online.

Many stores will even allow the use of store coupons for clearance items. This is the ideal time to use coupons, other discounts, and gift cards. It's possible to even acquire some items for free!

ACTION STEP: The next time you go shopping, bypass the merchandise in the front of the store and head straight for the clearance racks in the back. You might be surprised by what you'll find!

LOOK INTO
LOYALTY PROGRAMS

Many stores offer loyalty cards to frequent shoppers. With Kohl's, for example, customers can earn free credit to put toward future purchases. This is an easy way to score deeper discounts or even free items, but these discount programs should come with a caveat: because customers can earn more rewards by spending more, I have found that it often encourages unnecessary spending. If you already struggle with a spending problem, loyalty cards might not work in your favor. If you have to pay for a rewards card, be sure that you will use it enough to cover the cost.

ACTION STEP: For the stores you *already frequent*, check into whether they offer a loyalty program. For example, Target offers the REDcard, which will allow you to earn rewards or get discounts by being connected to your debit account (it's not a credit card!). If you find these reward cards lead to unnecessary spending, cut them up!

PROVIDE FOR HEALTH-CARE NEEDS

With health-care costs skyrocketing the past several decades, many families have found themselves in medical debt—or even avoiding doctors' visits because they can't afford to go.

Being a stay-at-home mom comes with worthwhile sacrifices, but your health and the health of your family shouldn't be one of them!

Thankfully, there are some viable ways to save on the costs of health care. This chapter will introduce you to some out-of-the-box ways to do just that.

HOP ON A HEALTH-SHARE PLAN

With the rising costs of insurance premiums in recent years, health-share plans have come into popularity at an unprecedented rate. Although some of these plans have been around for more than two decades, the general population is just now learning about this cost-effective alternative to traditional health insurance.

Our family first discovered health-share plans when I began blogging. Many of my blogging colleagues have been using these plans for years. Health-share plans are an ideal alternative to insurance for those who are self-employed (like bloggers), but they are also a way for those who are employed to save if employers do not offer affordable health-insurance benefits.

Four main health-share plan companies are on the market today. Note that most of these require that members adhere to the Christian faith, although some are more lenient with that requirement than others. These are the health-share plan companies:

- Samaritan Ministries: samaritanministries.org
- Christian Healthcare Ministries: chministries.org
- Medi-Share: mychristiancare.org
- Liberty HealthShare: libertyhealthshare.org

A downside to health-share plans is that most do not cover pre-existing conditions—at least for the first year, if not the first several years of membership.

ACTION STEP: Check into all the above health-share plans, and view the eligibility requirements as well as the costs of the plans. Evaluate whether switching to one of these would save you money on health-care expenses.

SAVE ON MEDICAL EXPENSES

When our family recently switched to a health-share plan, I stumbled upon MDsave (mdsave.com) while looking at ways to lower the up-front costs of medical bills. MDsave is a national website that allows you to buy medical tests, procedures, and therapies from a network of hospital providers at a discounted rate. MDsave boasts that average customers save $345 per procedure by using their site.[1] Purchases from MDsave can be applied to insurance deductibles, and customers can use HSA/FSA funds as well. MDsave also provides financing for those who are still not able to afford the up-front costs of their offerings. They also offer coupon codes on a regular basis, usually coinciding with holidays.

Note that the uninsured might be able to get deeper discounts than even what they might find via MDsave. Many hospitals, doctors' offices, and other medical facilities will give discounts to those who have no health insurance. Ours gives discounts of forty percent for "cash-pay" patients! Those who use health-share plans are considered cash pay because, technically, health-share plans are not insurance.

ACTION STEP: Check out mdsave.com to determine whether this website can be useful to your family's health-care needs.

USE PRESCRIPTION DISCOUNT CARDS

Have you ever gotten a prescription discount card in the mail? I have in the past, thinking they were junk. My mom decided to try one out, though, and it worked! That little card ended up saving her hundreds of dollars in the cost of prescription drugs.

My husband and I now use one of these cards too. When you get them in the mail, don't throw them away—use them!

ACTION STEP: Hold on to prescription discount cards you get in the mail, and use them to get discounts on drugs the next time you need them. Our family has used goodrx.com and savnet4 liberty.com (for Liberty HealthShare members). Others we haven't used that I found are refillwise.com and wellcardrx.com.

EYE ALTERNATIVE EYE CARE

Wouldn't it be awesome if we all had twenty-twenty vision? In reality, not many of us do. Will and I both have terrible vision, so glasses, contact lenses, and contact care are musts for us. So far, one of our four children has glasses as well. We will keep praying the others won't need them, but genetics does not seem to be in their favor!

We currently have vision insurance, but there are several ways to save on eye care even if you don't. Check into the following:

America's Best Contacts & Eyeglasses: America's Best (americasbest.com) is a nationwide, low-cost eye-care chain that my parents used when I was a child. They didn't have vision insurance, but my sister and I needed glasses. Our parents drove us to America's Best an hour each way, but it was worth it because, at the time, they were able to purchase a membership that included eye exams for the next ten years! At this writing, you can join their Eyecare Club, which includes eye exams for three years as well as discounts on glasses and contacts. Walmart and many warehouse stores also offer eye clinics at what is usually a more discounted rate than stand-alone optometry offices.

Coastal.com: This online eyeglasses and contacts store gives deep discounts and will occasionally give away free pairs of glasses! You must have your prescription before ordering.

Hubble Contacts: Hubble (hubblecontacts.com) is a contact lens subscription service. At this writing, you can get your first box of contacts for the cost of shipping. The service boasts that you can get your contacts each month for about one dollar per day, and you can cancel at any time. (Note: At this writing, it was still significantly cheaper to purchase contact lenses through America's Best.)

1-800 Contacts: 1-800 Contacts (1800contacts.com) claims that they will beat any competitor's price, so it would be wise to compare the prices of America's Best (if it's available to you), Hubble, and 1-800 Contacts to get the best deal.

Discount cards: Our family uses our SavNet (savnet4liberty .com) card to get a discount on eye care, but this is only available to Liberty HealthShare members. Another source I found online is wellcardrx.com/vision-care, which seems to work similar to prescription drug discount cards. Inquire whether your health-care program or insurance company offers anything like this.

ACTION STEP: Take an hour or two to price-compare the above options for eye exams, glasses, and contacts. Choose the most affordable route based on your findings.

VISIT A DENTAL SCHOOL

When it comes to dental health, regular checkups and cleanings can make a world of difference. But dental insurance is often hard to come by, and paying out of pocket for regular dental maintenance can get costly.

Dental schools will often offer checkups and cleanings at much more affordable rates, and the work is supervised by instructors. Sometimes you can also find coupons for dental procedures in sales flyers or online. When we were living on a low income and didn't have dental insurance, I used coupons to get my teeth cleaned.

ACTION STEP: Search online to find any dental schools in your area. Call the schools to inquire if they offer any free or affordable cleanings. Also, begin to scout for coupons you can use for dental needs, or check out wellcardrx.com/dental-care-savings.

SMILE YOUR WAY TO STRAIGHTER TEETH

I've never worn braces, but when I was writing this book, we found out that our oldest daughter needs them. Braces aren't cheap! A friend told me she used Smile Direct Club (smiledirectclub.com) as a more affordable alternative to braces. Smile Direct Club sends customers kits to take molds of their teeth at home. Smile Direct Club will then use the molds to make invisible aligners that you wear instead of braces. Everything comes through the mail.

At first glance, it sounds like Smile Direct Club will risk user error, but it's a fraction of the price of traditional braces, so it might be worth exploring.

ACTION STEP: If a family member needs braces, check out Smile Direct Club. It might be a viable option for you!

CANCEL YOUR GYM MEMBERSHIP

I want to start this with the disclaimer that I don't believe gym memberships are a waste of money. In fact, my husband currently has a gym membership. After Will turned forty last year, he experienced some alarming heart symptoms. He went to a cardiologist for a full workup of his heart health. The doctor advised that Will change his diet and do all he could to fit in exercise.

Our income has increased enough that a gym membership for my husband fits in our budget. However, if you are reading this book, I am assuming you want to do all you can to trim unnecessary areas of your spending to give your family enough financial margin for you to stay home with your kids.

If you or your spouse has a gym membership but you are still struggling to make ends meet, it might be time to cancel it. But how will you then find the motivation to exercise without a gym membership? Here are four ideas:

Take walks, jog, or ride a bike around your neighborhood. I've never been a runner, but I do enjoy walks and bike rides. A bonus is that you can do these with your kids! If you go alone, try listening to a podcast or music to keep you motivated.

Enlist accountability from a friend. I'm an extrovert, so I thrive around people. Exercising alone is hard for me! If the same is true for you, ask if any friends or neighbors would be willing to meet up with you to run, walk, or bike several times per week.

Invest in some low-cost exercise equipment. It's almost always possible to find exercise bikes, treadmills, elliptical machines, and hand weights on Craigslist, OfferUp, Letgo, and at thrift stores and yard sales. Discount stores Ross and T.J.Maxx often sell small exercise gear as well. You can set up an in-home gym with these—*but only buy them if you will use them!*

Try workout DVDs or free YouTube videos—or join a low-cost online "gym." Before we had kids, I kept fit with a series of exercise DVDs called *The Firm*. Now, I use an affordable online gym called Fit2B (fit2b.us/?ref=35). Fit2B provides tummy-safe (for ladies with a postpartum complication called a *diastasis recti*), low-impact fitness from a Christian instructor. The teacher, Beth Learn, is incredibly empathetic to mamas who have little time to work out. She encourages you to do what you can with what you already have in your home. It's not uncommon to see her demonstrating weight lifting using two canned goods instead of dumbbells, and she even has some routines that incorporate movements while holding babies!

ACTION STEP: If you have a gym membership but can't afford it, drop it today! Then brainstorm which of the above ideas will work for you.

Housing and vehicles are undoubtedly two of the biggest expenses anyone will ever have. Our family knows all too well the mistakes of purchasing a home before being ready. In 2012, we lost a home to foreclosure after trying to sell it for four years. After the Great Recession, the house had lost so much value that it was then worth less than what we owed on it. We look back and think, *If only we hadn't been in a rush to be homeowners, we could have avoided this mess.*

The good news is that there are many ways to save on housing—whether you are renting or plan to buy a home. In addition, you don't have to be a slave to a high car payment. By minimizing the stress of housing and vehicle payments, you will be well on your way to the financial breathing room that will allow you to stay home with your kids.

COUNT THE COSTS OF HOME OWNERSHIP

Our parents' generation had the mentality that renting a home equated to pouring money down the drain. After all, you get nothing back when you rent, but when you pay a mortgage, you are building equity. In a perfect economy, you will always be able to sell your home a few years after buying it and turn a profit.

But the Great Recession taught those of us born in the late-1970s to mid-1980s that even the most ideal economy will not last forever. Even millennials who came into adulthood after the recession witnessed some of its effects.

The truth is that unless you can afford the many costs of home ownership, it's best to wait until you can before purchasing a home. Home ownership is an investment of both time and money that does not stop when you've signed the closing papers and have the keys to the home in your hand.

The following are costs that homeowners incur that renters don't have to think twice about:

Major repairs: Roofs, HVACs, and hot water heaters are the three biggest costs of home ownership. Roofs last fifteen to thirty years and cost anywhere from $5,000 to $10,000 to replace. HVACs last fifteen to twenty years and cost upward of $4,000 to replace. Hot water heaters last eight to twelve years and cost $1,000 to $3,000 to replace, depending on if they have a tank (cheaper) or are tankless.

Basic home maintenance and repairs: Replacing air-vent filters, cleaning out the kitchen sink garbage disposal, cleaning range hood filters, repairing garage doors, replacing cabinet and door hardware, fixing broken plumbing, vacuuming refrigerator coils, and more are all tasks in which a homeowner must invest time and money.

HOA fees: Not all homes have a homeowners' association (HOA), but if your subdivision does, you'll be required to pay a fee monthly, quarterly, or annually. If the neighborhood you are eyeing comes with amenities like pools, walking trails, clubhouses, and tennis courts, your HOA fees will come with a hefty price tag.

Yard maintenance: You have to invest time into cutting the grass and weeding the flower beds. The costs of gas for lawn mowers, mulch for flower beds, any yard decor, soil for gardens, and the plants themselves can add up to hundreds (if not thousands) of dollars each year.

ACTION STEP: Before purchasing your next home, weigh the costs of home ownership. Will the home need a costly repair within the next few years? Can you afford basic home maintenance and yard work? Does the home come with HOA dues? And can you manage all of this on just your husband's income? Include all these factors in the price of the home.

RENT UNTIL YOU CAN AFFORD A HOME

This sounds counterintuitive and isn't the advice our parents' generation followed, but times have changed. Unless you can afford the expenses that come with home ownership (see "Count the Costs of Home Ownership" on page 158), then I firmly believe it's best to rent until you can.

While the price of rent is skyrocketing, you will be digging yourself into a deeper hole if you buy before you are ready. Will and I purchased our first home in 2006—just two years before the economic crash. In retrospect, we should have rented longer and saved for a larger down payment, which would have prevented us from eventually being stuck with an underwater mortgage and a home we couldn't sell during one of the worst economic crises in our nation's history.

If you are looking for an affordable place to rent, don't forget to negotiate. If it's time to renew your lease, don't be shy about asking for a discount. The worst your landlord can say is no, but he or she might surprise you and say yes, which can give you a little more breathing room until you can create more income for your family—from home.

ACTION STEP: If you are currently renting and are considering buying a home, think twice. Continue renting until you can afford all the expenses of home ownership on a single income. If you currently own your home and are having a hard time affording your mortgage payment and basic home maintenance and repairs at the same time, consider selling it and renting until you are better able to afford home ownership. Seek the advice of a financial-planning coach on how to best allocate the profits you make.

NEGOTIATE

When it comes to housing and vehicles, don't be afraid to negotiate! This is especially true when buying a home. Most sellers price their houses with enough wiggle room for the buyer's real estate agent to negotiate a better deal. That said, part of home pricing depends on current market trends. If it's a seller's market, you might not be able to negotiate as much as when it's a buyer's market. But it never hurts to ask for a lower price!

When it comes to renting, the cost of rent at apartment complexes and homes managed by rental services might be firm, but if you rent from an individual, you'll be more likely to negotiate a better deal. This is exactly what our family did when we were securing rental housing back in 2009. We had found a townhouse listing on Craigslist, but at the listed price of $850 per month, we'd be left with less than $1,000 per month to cover food, utilities, and unforeseen expenses. After viewing the home, I e-mailed the landlord to ask if she would accept $800 per month. To my surprise, she did. We ended up renting that townhouse for four years at the reduced rate—saving $2,400 in the process.

> **ACTION STEP:** The next time you're in the market for a new home or car, don't pay asking price. Negotiate for a better deal!

FLEX YOUR LOCATION

If you're not limited to a specific town or suburb within driving distance to your husband's work, your church, and amenities, flex your location search in order to save more on a home. Sometimes driving five minutes outside a city's limits will save you thousands of dollars both in the price of the home and in tax monies.

Where we live, for example, there are two local school districts. Both offer good schools, but one district is more desirable than the other. Homes in that school district, in turn, are a lot costlier than homes in the other district. Buying in the more desirable district can be good for resale value, but if you homeschool your children or send them to private school, you might be able to get more house for your money by flexing your location.

ACTION STEP: If you do not need to be in a certain area for schools or work, flex your location when searching for a home. You might save thousands of dollars by being willing to move outside your town's city limits or by moving to the next town over.

CHECK INTO COMMUNITY SERVANT DISCOUNTS

If you or your husband is currently a teacher, firefighter, nurse, EMS worker, or police officer, some home-buying incentives may be available to you. Check out the U.S. Department of Housing and Urban Development website for a government program that will subsidize community servants who meet certain income requirements.

ACTION STEP: If you or your spouse is a community servant, check out the U.S. Department of Housing and Urban Development website to inquire whether your family qualifies for home-buying discounts at hud.gov.

CONSIDER A HOME'S RESALE VALUE

When you are purchasing a house, don't forget to consider the home's resale value. This was a mistake Will and I made when we purchased our first home in 2006. We didn't consider then that the house we loved would not be very marketable when we wanted to sell it down the road. Why not? It only had two bedrooms and no garage. Homes with three bedrooms and garages open the floodgates of potential buyers—even compared to two-bedroom homes with the same square footage.

All the following affect a home's resale value:

Number of bedrooms: As stated above, homes with three or more bedrooms sell faster.

Storage space: Homes with garages are likely to sell faster than those without them.

Lot size: Homes with larger lots sell faster than ones with smaller lots in the same neighborhood—even if the homes are the same size.

Curb appeal: Houses with well-maintained, landscaped yards are more likely to sell than those without them. If you're purchasing a home with an unsightly yard, be prepared to invest both time and money in landscaping efforts. Everyone will need to at least maintain yard work, but you'll have a leg up if you purchase a home with an already maintained yard.

Age of roof, HVAC, and water heater: Roofs last anywhere from fifteen to thirty years. HVAC systems last between fifteen to twenty

165

years. Hot water heaters last eight to twelve years. If you are purchasing a home with older models of any of these and don't plan to stay in the home forever, keep in mind that you might need to replace one or all of them before selling the home in order to get the best price for the house.

Location: Homes in desirable school districts and close to shopping, hospitals, and schools will sell better than those off the beaten path or in school districts that fare lower in national and state rankings. Homes on cul-de-sacs within a neighborhood sell better as well.

Neighborhood amenities: Homes in neighborhoods with pools, recreation centers, and walking trails sell better than those in neighborhoods with no amenities.

Size of home for neighborhood: Smaller or medium-size homes in a neighborhood with larger homes will be able to get more money per square foot than the largest homes in the neighborhood.

Upgrades: Homes with no upgrades—like wood floors, granite countertops, and crown molding—in a neighborhood full of homes with these upgrades will be less likely to sell at a premium price. That said, it's unwise to invest in upgrades that will price your home out of your current neighborhood. If your home is the only home in the neighborhood with upgrades, it is unlikely your home will assess for the tax value you need to sell the house for the price you might desire. It's best to evaluate home upgrades in light of what the other homes in your area offer.

ACTION STEP: The next time you are thinking about purchasing a home, weigh the home's future resale value. You might not be able to check off all the items above, but aim to purchase a home that includes at least some of them!

EVALUATE HOUSING UPGRADES

At this writing, Will and I are considering when (if ever) we should move to a slightly larger home. We have four children and know that our current home might not be as comfortable when the three girls are all teenagers and our son is a tween.

As we are scoping out the housing market, it's become apparent that you will pay more for cosmetic upgrades like crown molding, granite countertops, stainless steel appliances, and wood or laminate flooring.

While these upgrades do make a home look beautiful, it's important to crunch numbers and truly evaluate whether the cost of rolling these amenities into your mortgage is worth it. Since you will be paying interest on these items over a fifteen- to thirty- year period (unless you purchase a home in cash, which is possible but not attainable for the masses), you will end up paying more for them than what they appear up front. For some upgrades, it might make more sense to wait and later add them on yourself (or hire an independent contractor to do them).

When you are considering the cost of upgrades—whether during the home-search stage or when you're ready for some home renovations—also consider the home's resale value (see "Consider a Home's Resale Value" on page 165).

ACTION STEP: The next time you're in the market for a new home, consider the cost of rolling upgrades into your mortgage. If you are buying used, it might make sense—especially if you can purchase a home with upgrades for the same price as a home without them. But if you are building a new home, weigh the pros and cons of doing so with upgrades that you might end up paying for over decades.

PLACE KIDS IN THE SAME BEDROOM

There is no rule that says your children—especially those of the same gender—cannot share a room. But our American culture has ingrained this false perception into our brains, and we have bought into the lie that we are depriving our children unless they each have their own space.

Since I grew up sharing a room with my younger sister, I've never felt the need for our children to have their own rooms. When our three girls were babies and toddlers, we lived in a two-bedroom townhouse. We had no other choice but for them to share a room. We purchased a bunk bed for our two oldest girls off a Facebook buy/sell/trade group, and our third daughter slept in her crib.

When we moved to a four-bedroom home, our daughters were one, three, and five. We realized we could maximize our new home's space by keeping all three girls together. For the first four years we lived in the home, they shared a room. Not until we added a new baby to our family (a son) did we split up the girls. At this writing, our middle two girls share a room, and our oldest daughter and the baby share. We use the fourth bedroom as a home office. Before the baby arrived, we used the third bedroom as a guest room and storage area for the kids' out-of-season clothing.

An added bonus of having children share bedrooms is the character lessons it instills in their hearts. We can teach children from an early age that the world does not revolve around them by providing ample opportunities for them to share. I had no trouble transitioning to sharing a dorm room with my roommate in college because I had spent my childhood sharing a room with my sister.

ACTION STEP: Does your house feel cramped? Do you long for a guest room or home office? Try having your children share a room. Or if you feel compelled to downsize, consider a home that offers fewer bedrooms than your current home. Yes, your children will have to share, but if it saves you hundreds of dollars per month in mortgage payments and will allow you to achieve your dream of staying home with your kids, then it might be worth it!

AVOID MAKING HOME INSURANCE CLAIMS

Homeowner's insurance isn't like health insurance; it's not meant to be used for every single minor home repair. In fact, the insurance company most likely will *not* cover small repairs. And when you *do* make a claim, your insurance company may raise their rates or even drop you as a client. Yes, if you own a home, you must have homeowners' insurance, but this type of insurance is for large, catastrophic damages to your home (think: the roof needs to be replaced because of a hail storm).

One week after we moved into our home, a pipe leak caused a wall in our living room to buckle. The insurance adjuster came, and even though we ended up paying for the repairs out of pocket, the claim still showed in our record. Two weeks later, the toilet in an upstairs bathroom flooded overnight, causing the ceiling in our kitchen to cave in. This was a *major* repair that would have cost us thousands of dollars without insurance. But because we had made two claims so close together, our insurance company dropped us! This resulted in us needing to secure a new insurance company, which raised our rate.

ACTION STEP: Save all claims for major damages. Otherwise, you might see the cost of your policy increase—or you could lose coverage.

BUNDLE CAR AND HOME INSURANCE

Many insurance agencies will lower the price of both car and home insurance if you purchase them together. Bundling these can save hundreds of dollars in the long run. If your agency doesn't offer this perk, it might be time to shop around for a new one.

ACTION STEP: Inquire whether your insurance company will bundle your car and home insurance for a rate lower than purchasing them separately. If your agency doesn't, shop around for an insurance company that will bundle to save you money.

EXTEND THE LIFE
OF YOUR VEHICLE

My dad has always been a stickler for car maintenance. He taught me that nothing wears out a car faster than missing oil changes, not regularly checking (and replenishing) fluid levels, and ignoring the fact that your vehicle needs regular care to last.

You should change your car's oil every three to six months or every 3,000 miles (whichever comes first). If you're brave (or maybe enlist the help of your husband), you can save a significant amount of money by changing your own oil. My dad did this all throughout my childhood. If you're not the handy type, then at least search for coupons. Many auto-parts stores and big chain mechanic shops offer these.

Maintaining your car's tires is also vital for its long-term use and safety. Tires are extremely expensive, but you can extend their life by keeping them inflated to proper levels, rotating them, and making sure the front end of your car is aligned.

In addition to regular car maintenance, limiting your car's usage will also make it last longer. Do you live in a pedestrian-friendly community with stores, parks, schools, and churches nearby? If so, try walking to these destinations instead of driving. You and your family will get fresh air, exercise, and extend the life of your vehicle in the process. When we take long trips, we try to budget for the cost of a rental vehicle when possible because it extends the life of our vehicle.

These small investments will add up over time and save you costlier car repairs (or replacements altogether).

ACTION STEP: Set up a regular car maintenance schedule, and stick to it! Find a downloadable vehicle maintenance tracker in the bonus content for this book at thehumbledhomemaker.com/sahm-book-freebies and use the password *icanstayhomewithmykids*.

BUY YOUR NEXT VEHICLE WITH CASH

Will and I didn't own a vehicle when we moved to North Carolina. It took us two years to purchase my parents' old (but reliable) minivan. The freedom we felt when we made that final payment was exhilarating, and we set a goal to buy our next vehicle in cash. It seemed an insurmountable dream at the time, but we were able to do just that in 2014. Then, in 2016, we bought a second vehicle in cash.

Here is how we did it:

We didn't shy away from driving an older, used vehicle. We drove an older minivan for years, even as we watched friends driving around newer, nicer vehicles. When someone rear-ended me, our insurance company totaled the minivan. However, the defects were purely cosmetic; the engine still ran fine. We negotiated with the insurance company to keep the van and for them to pay us a lesser amount of money in lieu of hauling it away. That van got us from point A to point B for two more years!

We avoided brand-new, pricier models. Brand-new cars lose their value as soon as you drive them off the lot, so we stuck to no-frills vehicles that were newer but not *new*.

We shopped around. Will and my dad drove several hours to check out vehicles, and for one of them, we ended up buying a former rental car. This gave us the best bang for our buck!

The bottom line when it comes to car shopping is to forego trying to keep up with the Joneses. Don't deny yourself the freedom of not having a car payment!

ACTION STEP: Avoid a car payment on your next vehicle by saving *now* to buy that car in cash. Work on the above steps to make it happen. Imagine how much not having a car payment can bolster your stay-at-home mom budget!

CHECK OUT AUTO AUCTIONS AND RENTAL VEHICLES

When I was a teenager, my dad frequented auto auctions with a mechanic friend of his. In fact, one of the first cars I called "my own" was once a police car. My dad purchased a 1992 Crown Victoria from a police car auction. It was boxy, white, and so huge that my friends called it "the boat," but it got me from point A to point B and kept me safe in the process. It was also an incredibly frugal find. Look for auto auctions at carauctionnetwork.com.

Having said all that, there is an art to buying a car at an auto auction, and I don't recommend going into it blindly. Do your research before venturing into the world of auto auctions.

As an alternative to an auto action, inquire at used car dealerships about buying rental vehicles. Our minivan was a rental, and we purchased it for a phenomenal price when it was only a year old!

ACTION STEP: If buying a car at an auction interests you, research the feasibility of doing so in your area. Don't go into this type of car buying blindly, but do consider if it you want to get a vehicle at a good rate.

Over the past several years, I've become passionate about teaching women how they can create more income from home. I've witnessed firsthand what a complete life changer this has been for our family, and I see so much potential for today's stay-at-home mom to bring in more money for her family.

Many women are able to stay at home with their kids without bringing in a penny. You may be one of them. But if you aren't, don't dismay. Start applying the money-saving tips in this book, and dive into this chapter. You might have to expand your definition from stay-at-home mom to work-at-home mom, but either way you can achieve the dream of staying home with your kids!

DETERMINE YOUR PURPOSE

Does your family need just a little extra money for wiggle room, or are you barely surviving on your husband's income and need to earn as close to a full-time income from home as possible? These are two very different scenarios, and answering the question *What is my purpose?* will help you establish which type of work-at-home mom avenue to take. Knowing your purpose in creating more income helps you stay focused. For example, if your goal is to make some fun money to satisfy your craving for gourmet coffee, then a side job that brings in a little extra will do the trick. But if you're living at or below the poverty level, you'll need to think more creatively about how to generate a longer-term, viable income for your family.

When Will and I started creating more income for our family, we dove headfirst into any and every way to make a little extra money. But none of these added up to the significant income source we needed. Eventually, I homed in on blogging, which has become our family's main source of income. Will and I now run thehumbledhomemaker.com together.

Remember that time is money. It's easy to make a few extra bucks here and there by filling out online surveys, using certain search engines (like Swagbucks.com), and doing reviews. If you just need a little extra, this might be your answer (check out money savingmom.com for some suggestions), but these will not add up to much money per hour, so evaluate your true needs before pursuing these side gigs with abandon. It might be that you need something more.

> ACTION STEP: Take a few minutes and brainstorm your purpose in wanting to create more income for your family through a work-at-home mom gig. Pray and ask God to give you wisdom in what area to pursue. Download a free printable brainstorming sheet as part of the bonus content for this book at thehumbledhomemaker.com/sahm-book-freebies. Use the password *icanstayhomewithmykids*.

DISCOVER YOUR STRENGTHS

When you're seeking the best fit for creating more income from home, it's important to utilize your strengths. What works for your friend or neighbor (or me!) won't necessarily work for you. When we work out of our God-given talents, we will be so much more fruitful in our ventures.

I recommend taking these personality assessments: the Myers-Briggs Type Indicator (MBTI), the Enneagram, and the Four Temperaments Test. Once you know your personality type, read up on the usual strengths and weaknesses of those types. This will help you cross out certain types of income generators (in my case, I would be terrible at data entry) and begin to explore others (in my case, it would be anything involving people or language skills). I also recommend taking the StrengthsFinder test, which will give you an even better look into what types of work fit your gifts.

ACTION STEP: Take free versions of the Myers-Briggs (16personalities.com/free-personality-test), Four Temperaments (temperamentquiz.com), and the Enneagram (yourenneagram coach.com) tests online. I recommend paying the small fee to find your top five strengths at the StrengthsFinder test (gallupstrengths center.com) when you can afford it. Use these as a starting point to discovering your God-given gifts.

SET UP YOUR BUSINESS

It's important to treat your at-home business like a business from the start—because it is! I made the mistake of treating my blog like a hobby for the first couple years I ran it. Even if you're afraid to dream of this side gig creating enough income for you to achieve your goal of staying home with your kids (with financial freedom), heed my advice and take the following steps early on. You won't be sorry!

Set up a separate bank account for your business. When I first started blogging, I kept all the money in our personal account. After all, I thought it was a hobby and was afraid to dream of more. But because I hadn't kept a faithful accounting of my increasing income, we ended up getting a hefty tax bill. Track every penny from day one—and do so in an account separate from your personal monies.

Stick to office hours. If you have small children, the obvious time to work is while they are sleeping. This is how I started. Later, we were able to hire a part-time mother's helper so I could have some daytime hours to work as well. Working during set hours will help your work and personal lives not bleed into each other, which can make for one really stressed-out mama!

Keep track of tax write-offs. If you use your phone and Internet for your business, part of these bills can be written off your taxes. Home-office space, travel, and supplies can also be deducted. That brings me to the next point:

183

Hire a bookkeeper or a certified public accountant (CPA) to prepare your taxes. I know I am suggesting you spend money here, and I realize that is not something you may be able to do at first. But as soon as you are able, I highly recommend you hire someone to help you do your taxes. Your taxes will be more complicated when you are self-employed, and investing in a professional to help you will save you money in the long run.

Determine your business type. If it's just you, you are probably going to file your taxes as a sole proprietor. Once your income increases, you might look into filing as a Limited Liability Company (LLC). This protects you in the event of a lawsuit. One day you might be able to set up your business as an S corporation, which has certain tax benefits for those who are earning above a certain amount. If your at-home business is direct sales or a multilevel marketing venture, your upline sponsor should be able to help you with this. If not, I recommend talking to a CPA.

Join a business support group. Brilliant Business Moms, iBloom in Business, and Christy Wright's Business Boutique are all networks for Christian women in business that I have utilized at some point in my work-at-home mom journey. Also, check your local Chamber of Commerce for their offerings. Consider attending a professional conference like Business Boutique, which is perfect for female entrepreneurs. This has been one of my favorite conferences to attend over the past few years.

ACTION STEP: If you're ready to try a work-at-home mom gig, start by setting up a separate bank account just for your business (make sure to discuss this with your spouse first!). Then work your way through the other steps to set up your business.

MAKE AND SELL

Many moms generate income from home by selling homemade items on online marketplaces like Etsy.com and HyenaCart.com, at local craft shows, and even via personal websites.

After she became a mom, my friend Erin, a nurse and lactation counselor by trade, began making lactation cookies to help breastfeeding mamas increase their milk production. She and her friends enjoyed them so much that she decided to make a business out of baking them for postpartum moms. I enjoyed her "Mama Bear Milk Boosters" cookies for the first few months after my fourth child was born. This venture merges Erin's passion and gifting—and allows Erin's not to miss time with her son.

In the same vein, those gifted with other talents such as painting, pottery, and ceramics might want to consider how those can become business ventures. When Illinois mom Joy discovered she had a knack for the art of face painting, she created The Joy of Face Painting, sharing her talents at children's birthday parties and other events.

ACTION STEP: Do you enjoy baking, sewing, or crafting? Brainstorm items you can make and begin selling to earn a profit for your family (without leaving home!).

FIND FREELANCE WORK

When Will and I were trying to make it on a low income, I began freelance writing for my local newspaper. The gig helped me re-hone my rusty writing skills, and it also eventually led to my starting a blog (which became our family's main income source a few years later). I have also done freelance editing work, and my husband has done freelance photography.

If you're interested in freelance writing or photography, pitch it to your local newspaper editor. It never hurts to ask! If you're interested in freelance editing, I recommend e-mailing your favorite bloggers with a job pitch or checking job postings on sites like Upwork.com, an online platform where freelancers can connect with businesses to find home-based work.

If you have graphic-design skills, check out freelance work on sites like Upwork or Fiverr (fiverr.com), or try selling your designs on Etsy. Bloggers and small-business owners pay freelance designers to create graphics like invitations, event posters, printables, e-book covers, and more. It never hurts to approach a business owner and offer your services.

ACTION STEP: Pitch to your local newspaper editor or your favorite blogger about freelance writing or editing. Check job listings at Upwork.com to see if any match your skill set.

START A BLOG

When I tell people our family makes a living by blogging, I get the funniest looks. Although this has been a viable livelihood for more than a decade now, most people still don't understand how it works.

Bloggers make money via several different income streams. Network advertising, sponsored posts, private sponsors, affiliate marketing, and product sales are the main ways. All of these income streams can make up a lucrative income.

Blogging isn't easy, though, and it's become more competitive through the years. Check out the short series I wrote on how to start a blog for yourself at thehumbledhomemaker.com/pick-my-brain.

ACTION STEP: If you're interested in starting a money-making blog, check out my blogging series and start to explore whether this is a possible business venture for you.

JOIN A DIRECT SALES COMPANY

Selling makeup through a direct sales company was my first dip into the ocean of entrepreneurial living. I tried this when Will and I were newlyweds. I was teaching full-time, but I thought direct sales might provide supplemental income for us. I was wrong. Because I'm *not* a natural salesperson, instead of making money, I ended up spending it in order to meet my required monthly sales quotas.

Direct sales wasn't a match for *me*, but it can be an incredibly fruitful income source and has been for many of my friends. With hundreds of direct sales companies in operation, it can be overwhelming to decide which one to join. Choose a company with products you are so passionate about that you would share them with others even if you didn't get paid.

ACTION STEP: Take some time to explore various direct sales opportunities on the market today—essential oils, health-care products, clothing, makeup, and more. Do you love any of these products so much that you would share about them even if you weren't making money? If so, you might consider joining up with one of these companies!

BECOME A VIRTUAL ASSISTANT

A virtual assistant (VA) is a remote administrative assistant, usually hired on a contract basis. As long as you have a computer, the Internet, and a phone, you don't need to leave home! VAs can work for individuals in other towns, in other states, or even in other countries.

One of my first attempts at creating more income for our family was by working as a VA for a blogger. I quickly discovered that I'm *not* cut out for VA work. Virtual-assistant work requires a lot of organization and can also be monotonous. This is great for those who are naturally organized or enjoy doing the same tasks again and again. With my personality, I get bored easily. While being a VA is the perfect job for some, it wasn't the job for me. Years later, I'm thrilled to have given several VAs jobs through my business.

ACTION STEP: If VA work interests you, check out the e-book *The Bootstrap* VA by Lisa Morosky and the Moms Work Hard (momsworkhard.com) e-course. These are great resources that detail how to become a successful VA.

TEACH OR TUTOR

When we were seeking to make extra money, both Will and I tutored students for a while. Tutoring—whether online or in person—is a good option for teachers or experts in certain subjects. Will also sold teaching tools through teacherspayteachers.com. This online marketplace allows teachers to buy and sell lesson plans, worksheets, and other activities. In addition to tutoring at a local elementary school when our firstborn was a baby, I taught Spanish to a homeschool family's children.

Consider if your knowledge or expertise is something others—children or adults—would be interested in learning. Teaching others to play musical instruments, create art, speak a foreign language, or learn computer skills all come to mind as possibilities. You can tutor one-on-one or in live workshops. An opportunity for online teachers that is surging in popularity is VIPKID (t.vipkid.com.cn). VIPKID allows stay-at-home parents to teach English to children in China during early-morning or late-night hours—while their own children are sleeping.

Another option can be creating an online course. Many of my blogging colleagues earn a full-time income through their online courses. From cooking courses to classes on health and wellness and even creating online fitness studios, moms are using their skill sets to educate others while earning an income from home. Teachable.com,

191

Thinkific.com, and CourseCats.com are three platforms for creating and selling your own online courses.

> **ACTION STEP:** Do you have a skill that others want to learn? Consider whether you can offer tutoring or teaching to others.

BUY AND RESELL

My grandmother embraced her entrepreneurial spirit out of a personal passion and necessity when she became a single mom. She spent her weekdays frequenting thrift stores and her weekends shopping yard sales to purchase inventory for her business. A lover of fine antiques and secondhand shopping, Granny turned her skills into a business that supported her for the rest of her life.

Many families today create extra income by buying and reselling secondhand items—clothing, toys, shoes, baby gear, furniture, home decor, books, and more—via eBay.com, Amazon.com, online yard sales, consignment shops, Craigslist.org, apps like OfferUp and Letgo, and BookScouter.com.

ACTION STEP: Do you have a love for thrifting? Brainstorm some ways you can turn this hobby into a business. Begin researching ways you can buy and sell items for a profit.

MANAGE SOCIAL MEDIA

After our second daughter was born, I started using cloth diapers. My favorite online store was a small start-up called Jack Be Natural. After building a relationship with the store owners through their Facebook page, they asked if I would be interested in *managing* the page. Not only did I get a discount on diapers, but they also paid me an hourly wage.

Because I'm naturally relational, running their Facebook page was a breeze. I worked as the social media manager at Jack Be Natural for about a year, until my blog grew to the point that I needed to focus on it full time.

ACTION STEP: If you think you have the personality to be a social media manager, I encourage you to take the initiative and contact some of your favorite small-business owners. For years now, several ladies have helped run my social media at thehumbledhomemaker.com, and there isn't a business owner I know who wouldn't mind extra support in this department.

EXPLORE EVENT PLANNING

Do you have a knack for throwing parties and bringing people together? Maybe event planning is part of your calling! From wedding receptions to baby showers to birthday parties, there are families who will pay individuals to plan events they don't have time to put together.

ACTION STEP: Are you good at party planning? Consider volunteering to plan an event for a friend who will give you a good testimonial so you can begin an event-planning side gig.

DOULA FOR BIRTHING MOMS

When I was pregnant with our second daughter, I became passionate about natural childbirth. We hired a doula, which is a childbirth assistant, to accompany my husband and me to the birth. Because of the support of my doula, I had a great natural childbirth. I went on to have two more natural births with my third and fourth children—both with the help of a doula.

I have several friends who are doulas. Certified birth doulas can charge upward of $700 to $800 (or more) per birth, and the time investment can be minimal. If you are empathetic in personality and passionate about natural childbirth, this might be an excellent fit for you. If you don't think you are able to attend births themselves, consider becoming a postpartum doula. They assist mothers in the early postpartum period by cooking, cleaning, and helping do whatever the new mother needs. This is probably not the best fit for a mom who still has young children at home, but it might be an ideal job for a stay-at-home mom whose children are in school during the day or for a mom with teenagers.

If breastfeeding is a passion of yours, you might also consider becoming a certified lactation counselor. Certification does not require as many hours as international board certified lactation consultants, but counselors are still able to charge for their services. I saw a lactation counselor several times after the birth of my son.

ACTION STEP: Check out Dona International (dona.org) and CAPPA (cappa.net), which both offer doula certification. Explore the costs involved in becoming certified and whether this might be a viable income source for you in the future. You might also look into becoming a certified lactation counselor via a CAPPA program.

As we come to the end of this book, I imagine your head might be spinning just a bit with all the different ways you have learned how to curb spending, save wisely, and create more income for your family from home. We've been on this journey together, and now it's your turn to take the tips you believe will best work for your family and begin implementing them in your life. Motherhood can be overwhelming, but when you bathe each day in prayer, focus on your goal of staying home with your kids, and take one step at a time, I believe you can get there.

One thing I used to tell myself (until it finally took root!) and have told my readers at *The Humbled Homemaker* for years is that God made you your children's mother because He knew you were the perfect mom for them. There might be days when you wonder if all your hard work is worth it, and I assure you: it is. Let's persevere together, Mama. Remember your "why." You can do this! You can stay home with your kids!

CHAPTER 1: CURB SPENDING

1. "911 Wireless Services," Federal Communications Commission, accessed October 18, 2018, https://www.fcc.gov/consumers/guides/911-wireless-services.
2. Trent Hamm, "Turn Off the Lights to Save Money . . . But How Much?" last modified August 26, 2014, http://www.thesimpledollar.com/how-much-money-does-turning-off-the-lights-really-save.
3. "Best Practices: Clothes Washer Tips," Energy Star, accessed October 18, 2018, https://www.energystar.gov/index.cfm?c=clotheswash.clothes_washers_ performance_tips.
4. Ibid.

CHAPTER 6: PROVIDE FOR HEALTH-CARE NEEDS

1. "MDsave: How It Works," MDsave, accessed October 18, 2018, https://www.mdsave.com/patients#patient-savings.

DON'T MISS ERIN'S FREE BONUS CONTENT!

Download Erin's printable resources for *You Can Stay Home with Your Kids!*

- Meal planning worksheet
- Price book worksheet
- Freezer cooking cheat sheet
- "Kids Eat Free" restaurant guide
- Vehicle maintenance tracker
- Brainstorming your purpose worksheet

Available at thehumbledhomemaker.com/sahm-book-freebies. Use the password *icanstayhomewithmykids.*

ACKNOWLEDGMENTS

When I wrote a blog post titled "Staying at Home with Your Kids When You Can Barely Afford It" in October 2012, I never would have dreamed it would go viral and that one day—many years later—lead to me writing this book.

At the time, our family was struggling to make ends meet. A few blogging friends knew that we were, and they encouraged me to be transparent with my readers. I can't pretend that my heart wasn't about to beat out of my chest and my fingers weren't trembling when I clicked "publish" on that post.

And, secretly, I hoped that no one would pay attention to it. Talking about financial struggles in the midst of my dream to stay home with my children was scary.

I was shocked to wake up tens of thousands of pageviews on that post. That post would go on to reach millions, with new readers continuing to stumble upon it nearly every single day—more than five years after I originally published it. While I had written it to encourage other mamas and to simply be authentic, I never dreamed that it would resonate with so many.

What I discovered was that I wasn't alone in my struggle or my desire to stay home with my kids. We were coming out of a recession. Was there someway, anyway that I could continue to stay home with our kids when we were barely making ends meet?

I learned that there was!

Without the following people, that post might have evaporated into the blogosphere all these years later. Instead, it morphed into the book you're now holding in your hands.

My Lord and Savior Jesus: You have put desires in our heart to glorify your name. You gave me the dream to write—and to stay home with my kids. Thank you, Lord, for helping me achieve both. In your sovereignty, you knew that writing would be the conduit through which I would be able to stay home! I pray that you are glorified through this book and through the motherhood journey of those who read it and implement the tips therein—so they, too, can stay home with their kids.

Will: Thank you for being open to me staying home with our kids. I know it hasn't always been easy, but I think we can both say it's been worth the sacrifices we've made. I love you!

My three girls and little boy: You are the reason why I want to stay at home. Penny pinching and late-night work-at-home mom gigs are so incredibly worth it to get to spend time with you four each and every day! I love you more than rainbows and to the moon and back.

Mom: You modeled what I saw as the perfect stay-at-home mom. Watching you stay home with me and my siblings gave me the desire to do the same with my children. Thank you! I love you!

Daddy: Thank you for placing importance on Mama staying at home with her kids. Having her there gave me a wonderful model to look up to. Your hard work made it happen. I love you!

Bill: You took a chance on a random blogger when you sent me that first email back in January 2014. Thank you for following the Lord's leading and for believing in me when I didn't believe in myself. Without you, this book would not be.

Molly: Thank you so much for approaching me about this book in 2015. I loved seeing how God worked through you finding my lactation cookie recipe on my blog during your maternity leave. I am so grateful for you. I hope you are enjoying being a stay-at-home mom!

Dawn, Tim, and the rest of the gift books team: Thank you so much for believing in this project and using your amazing editing, design, and marketing skills to make it happen. You all ROCK!

To all of you, I am forever grateful.

rin Odom is the founder of *The Humbled Homemaker*, a blog dedicated to grace-filled living and designed to equip and encourage mothers in the trenches. Her Southern charm and wealth of inspirational, practical content has drawn an audience of millions over the years. Erin and her husband, Will, live in the South, where they raise their four children. Follow Erin at thehumbledhomemaker.com.

JOURNAL

JOURNAL

_____

_____

_____

_____

_____

_____

_____

_____

_____

_____

_____

_____

_____

JOURNAL

JOURNAL

JOURNAL

JOURNAL

_____

_____

_____

_____

_____

_____

_____

_____

_____

_____

_____

_____

_____

JOURNAL

JOURNAL

JOURNAL

JOURNAL

_____

_____

_____

_____

_____

_____

_____

_____

_____

_____

_____

_____

_____

SIGN UP FOR ERIN'S FREE, 5-DAY VIDEO E-COURSE– EATING WELL ON A BUDGET!

Eating Well on a Budget is a five-day video course that will guide you from grocery stress to grocery savings! Sign up now to gain access to five video teachings, e-mail lessons, and free printables and worksheets. Learn more at eatingwellonabudget.com.

Confessions of a **Cloth Diaper** Convert

a simple, comprehensive guide to using cloth diapers

Erin Odom

CONFESSIONS OF A CLOTH DIAPER CONVERT

Ever feel like you're flushing your family's money down the toilet by how much you're spending on diapers? Erin Odom knows your pain!

When she had two babies in diapers, she made the switch to cloth diapers in order to pour much-needed funds back into her family's budget.

But, at first, she just wasn't sure she could make the switch:

- There were so many cloth diaper types on the market that she felt utterly confused.
- Her husband wasn't open to using cloth diapers.
- And she couldn't even afford the initial investment of cloth-diapering supplies.

But through it all, she persevered. She troubleshooted and experimented until cloth diapering became just as easy as using disposables.

More than seven years later, Erin has cloth diapered four children and saved her family thousands of dollars in the process.

Erin wrote *Confessions of a Cloth Diaper Convert* to help save others the time it took her to research and the frustration she experienced when she encountered cloth-diapering challenges.

Confessions of a Cloth Diaper Convert can help you overcome any cloth-diapering challenge. If you read it before you start, you may just eliminate any challenges all together!

Available on amazon.com.

Erin Odom grew up among the neatly manicured lawns of upper middle-class America but was thrown into low-income living during the economic crash. She was a stay-at-home mom, and even though she and her husband had no consumer debt, they were scrambling to make ends meet. Suddenly Erin found herself standing in line for food stamps and walking into bankruptcy court during the eighth month of her third pregnancy.

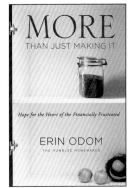

More Than Just Making It tells the story of the Odoms' breaking point as well as the secrets that led to their comeback. It took hard work, creativity, and faith in God's provision to reset their bank account as well as their hearts. In this book, Erin passes on the tips and habits that enabled her family to put thirty percent down on a home, pay cash for a minivan, and send their daughters to a private Christian school.

More Than Just Making It will encourage you to rise above your circumstances, empower you with money-saving tips, and reimagine the good life as God designed it.

Available in stores and online!